D0796949

The Fugitive's Sister

Linda Case

W & B Publishers
USA

W & B Publishers

For information:
W & B Publishers
Post Office Box 193
Colfax, NC 27235
www.a-argusbooks.com

ISBN: 9781942981367

Book Cover designed by Dubya
Author's photo by Jessica Nash
Printed in the United States of America

The Fugitive's Sister

The contents of *The Fugitive's Sister* is solely the point of view of Linda Case, and any and all information used is from her personal experience, court documents, newspaper articles and/or media interviews. Any reference to persons, places or events is from her own intimate involvement in the case and recollections thereof.

Author Linda Case and her sister, Becky, in 1949.

Though nothing can bring back the hour
Of splendor in the grass
Glory in the flower,
We will grieve not
Rather find strength
In what remains behind
.....Excerpt from "Ode to Immortality" by William
Wordsworth

In Loving Memory of My Beloved Son,
	Michael Wade Blakeman – November 10, 1960 – September 6, 1998

And My Beloved Brother,
	Dannie Robert Mayes – October 10, 1940 – November 10, 2002

Dedication

I dedicate this book to my beloved daughter, Sheri, without whom I would surely be dead! With all my thanks and love for the wonderful person you are. With deep gratitude for how good you are to me, how generous with your heart and time. You gave up your dream of opening a bed and breakfast in Mexico after years of planning and saving, and remained in Columbus for **six** long months in order to care for my entire household affairs while I was incarcerated. You cared for my 100lb. dog, Sonny Boy, my four cats, my mother who had been living with me and was suffering with Alzheimer's disease and mom's three cats! You put your life on hold, rounded up more evidence to clear me than my attorney, contacted friends and family for support, and maintained your beautiful positive attitude throughout. Most of all, you assured me every day, day after day for six months, that *everything was going to be all right*!

I wish you love, peace, joy, friends, happy endings, and a spouse who treasures you and treats you with tenderness, love and respect. You are amazing, exceptionally wonderful, and I am truly blessed to have you as my daughter **and** my best friend!!

With All My Love,
Mom

Acknowledgments

Many people will walk in and out of your life, but only *true* friends will leave footprints in your heart. Thanks with all my heart to my family, *true* friends, clients and even some strangers who called me their "hero." ALL have left their footprints in my heart forever.

My eternal gratitude to Johnnie Bernhard and Jeanie Loiacono of Loiacono Literary Agency for believing in me and for providing the opportunity for my story to be told.

Thanks to my brilliant friend and special reader/editor, Michele Pike for her expertise in working with me to turn my lump of coal into a sparkling diamond. Michele has been working as an editor and writer for eighteen years and is the author of the book, *How to Live an Exotic Life in an Ordinary World*.

Special love and thanks to my two daughters, Sheri Kent and Trisha Cardillo, their husbands, Albert Contreras and Tom Cardillo, Aunt Clara Dunlap, grandsons, Tyler Blakeman Compton, Travis Compton, Aaron Kurzweg, Tony Cardillo, granddaughters, HoneyMichelle Blakeman and Marlee Rose Blakeman, and great-grand-daughters, Ava Blakeman and Maxine Kurzweg. A special thank you to my kindred spirit, best friend and bridge partner, Betty Palestrant.

Special family includes: Kathleen Compton, Tara Margolin, Arielle Margolin, Pat Northup, Troy Dunlap, Natasha Mayes Dowling, Jack Mayes and Patricia Hosack. Friendship isn't about who you've known the longest, it's about those who came and never left your side. Those friends who never left: Lori Schaad, Ed Hurley, Todd Licklider, Tony Helmic, Cindy Davis, Honey Barnes, Ray Skonce, Hugh McCracken, Charles Weis, Jennifer Wagoner, Anna Armentrout, Phil and Sharon Reynolds, Carla Eaddy, Rezella Fraley, James Waddy, Tammy Lewis, Sylvia Lilley, Emmy Haji, Ginny Shoemaker, Ursula Holloway, Eileen Erwin, Dorris Wood, Billie Bahn, Martha and Bob Chilcote, Betty Mathias, Carolyn Sellers, Brian Hunt, Frona Call, Mickey Snead, Al and Eve Crego, Cathy Alberti, Tom Fletcher, Joyce Penn, Tom Martin, Amy Ritter, Teresa Shuler, Chuck Campbell.

Table of Contents

2008

- A Shred of Hope, *February 3*
- Guilty, Guilty, Guilty, *February 4-March 13*
- Flight Risk, *March 14*
- R& R, *March 16*
- My Sister is Missing, *March 18*
- Runaway Train Gathers Steam, *March 27*
- *America's Most Wanted, May 3*
- Box of Surprises, *July*
- A Slippery Slope, *August-September*
- As Good as it Gets, *October-December*

2009

- Lost and Broken
- U.S. Marshals' Visit, *March 9-27*
- Violated and Abused, *March 27-April 30*
- A Dream Renewed, *May 6*
- ABC Producer Visits, *May 26*
- Breakdown, *June-October*
- Happiness Arrives Early, *November-December*

2010

- Prep Time, *January*
- Do Me Twice, *February 5*
- Arrested! (Worst Day of My Life, continued), *February 12*
- Rude Awakening, *February 13*
- Valentine's Day Behind Bars, *February 14*
- Court Appearance, *February 16*
- Secrecy and Despair, *February 18-25*
- Jail Bait, *February 26*
- Life Behind Bars, *March*
- March Madness, *March 19-31*
- Along Came a Spider, *April*

Worst Day of My Life
February 12, 2010

Ten days before heading south to Mexico to realize my dreams and be near my best friend and daughter, I was arrested. At age 66, a grandmother with no prior criminal record of any kind, a SWAT team hauled me off to jail like a bag of common garbage!

***

There was still a lot of work to be done before heading south to Veracruz, Mexico, but I was so happy to finally be realizing my dreams: to live in a tropical climate, to be able to provide professional home care for my mother and, most of all, to be near my best friend and daughter, Sheri. So engrossed in my thoughts, I failed to see the unfamiliar black SUV that had been parked at a nearby corner for quite some time.

It was going to break my heart to leave my mother behind at Monterey Care Center – even though it would only be for a brief time, until I could return to Columbus, Ohio to take her to Mexico. Only in Mexico would we be able to afford an around-the-clock nurse for my mother. She was suffering with Alzheimer's disease, which was getting progressively worse, along with still recuperating from a broken hip and hip replacement surgery. In our south-of-the-border living arrangement, Sheri and her husband, Albert, would also be near to help with her care. I was overjoyed my mother was going to be able to spend her twilight years with her family and her three beloved cats.

Sheri and Albert were planning and had been saving money for the trip to Mexico for several years. Their dream plan was to open a Bed and Breakfast in Puerto Escondido after visiting briefly with Albert's family, whom he had not seen in more than ten years, in Veracruz. I would travel to Veracruz with them, get settled in Puerto Escondido, then fly back to Columbus and escort my mother down to join us. That was the plan.

A glance at the clock on the stove said it was almost 8:30 a.m. and time for me to stop daydreaming. I had almost finished my morning routine – feed the cats and dog, have my cup of ginseng tea followed by two cups of freshly-brewed Highlander Grogg coffee. Still in my robe, I looked out the large, kitchen bay window at the snow and wondered how in the world I would ever be able to get everything done in only ten days. As I sipped the last few drops of coffee, I superficially noticed the black SUV parked on the corner. A few minutes later, just like something out of the movies, five black vehicles pulled into the driveway in front of my house. A SWAT team of what seemed like a dozen officers, dressed in black with guns drawn, ran up to the front door and around the house to the back door.

"My God!" I said aloud, "What's happening?!"

The pack was led by Drew Shadwick, U.S. Marshal. When I opened the door, Marshal Shadwick rushed in and said loudly, "You are under arrest! Is anyone else in the house? Do you have any guns in the house?"

"No, no," I said.

My next thought was concern for my dog, Sonny Boy. "Please don't hurt my dog!" I pleaded. "He's very friendly and won't hurt anyone!" No sooner had I gotten the words out of my mouth when Sonny bounded into the room with a toy in his mouth. He thought we were all playing, and he wanted to play too.

The rest of the SWAT team was running through the house, upstairs, downstairs, with submachine guns drawn. I was never so frightened in my entire life.

"This is unbelievable," I said to Marshal Shadwick. "Why are you doing this to me?"

He replied, "Do you blame me?"

"Of course, I do," I continued. "You've been here before. You know I am a sixty-six year old grandmother with a dog and seven cats who wouldn't hurt a flea! This is totally unnecessary!"

As I was being handcuffed and my feet put in shackles, I asked, "Could I please get dressed and call my daughter?" Marshal Shadwick allowed a female officer to assist me in getting dressed but would not allow me to phone my daughter.

"Please don't let my dog or cats out!" I begged as several officers escorted me outside to their unmarked vehicle. "They are my family," I cried.

Three of the cats actually belonged to my mother who was currently recuperating from surgery at Monterey Care Center. I was grateful my mother was not present to see me dragged off like a common criminal.

The marshals took me to the Franklin County, Ohio, Courthouse where I was finger-printed and booked.

The Beginning of the End
November 9, 2002

Eight years earlier, on a crisp and sunny November afternoon in Buford, Georgia, I returned home from the local video store. I had just picked up a long night's worth of videos to help me get through the eve of my son's birthday. Michael was my first born and only son. Ever since he died, four years ago, I found it impossible to sleep the night before his birthday. So, as I had done for the previous four November 9ths, I planned to fill those empty hours by watching videos.

In 1996, I sold my business, Case Accounting and Tax Service, and moved from Ohio to California to be near my son, Michael, his children, and my daughter, Sheri, who was also living there at the time. After Michael's death in 1998, Sheri and I decided to relocate to Buford, Georgia where Trisha, my youngest daughter, and her husband and two children were living. I hated living so far away from my four grandchildren in California, but at least I was living near my two daughters and two other grandchildren in Georgia.

It was late afternoon when the phone rang. My brother, Dannie, was calling from his hospital bed at the James Cancer Center, a part of Ohio State University Hospital in Columbus. Dan was hospitalized for about ten weeks. Earlier this year, he'd been diagnosed with leukemia. After entering the hospital, he contracted cellulitis, an infection of the cells, which prevented treatment for the leukemia. Dan was crying hard on the phone.

"Hi Hon. Listen. You and Becky haven't gotten along for years, and I know you haven't spoken one word to her in almost four years. This really hurts Mom and me," Dan explained. "Now, don't speak, just listen to me."

"Remember when we were growing up? Every night, before Becky could go to sleep, Mom would make us forgive her for all the mean things she'd done to us all day?"

"Yes," I said. "Like the time Becky wanted to play with my metal toy cash register. I said, 'No, it has sharp edges and you might hurt yourself.' She sneaked it out of my closet anyway, fell on it, and cut a big gash in her leg. I got ten whacks with dad's belt when she lied and said I 'pushed' her. You got whacked with the belt a few times too! How about that time she tattled on you for smoking a cigarette? Adding insult to injury…not only did we get punished, but at the end of each day, we also were forced to forgive her! How fair is that?"

He continued, "Well, I want you to promise me that you'll forgive her, one more time, for what she did to you and your girls in Arizona just after Michael died. And, I want you to promise me you'll look out for her and Mom after I'm gone! You know how they have always depended on me to be there for them. Will you do that for me? Please?"

There was a note of urgency in his voice, and he was sobbing uncontrollably. I grabbed the closest chair as I felt my legs beginning to melt away. I had only seen my brother cry one other time in my entire life – at our father's funeral. I remember it distinctly because Dan really did not know how to cry. The sound he made was more of a whimper, with tears. It was so sad. Dan was a real macho kind of guy; he believed that "real men don't cry". This time was different. I was filled with dread as I realized Dan must believe that he is going to die soon.

"Of course I will," I said, "but quit talking about dying. You are NOT going to die…not for a long, long time. You're my big brother and you MUST get well…for all of us. I need you, too!" I love you. No more talk about dying. You get some rest and I'll talk to you tomorrow."

"I love you, too," he said. "Don't forget your promise," he added, as he hung up the phone.

I could hold my tears no longer; I began crying hysterically. The last time I saw Dan was in September. I used a week of my vacation time from work to travel up to Columbus to visit him in the hospital. He hated being there. His body was terribly swollen from the cellulitis, which kept him bed ridden. He begged the nurses to put him in a wheelchair, so he could be taken outside to smoke a cigarette. Of course, that just wasn't an option. On that trip, I spent every day visiting Dan with my mother. My mother was exhausted, but she would have crawled to the hospital to be with Dan if it had been necessary. Dan was her pride and joy, her first born, her only son. Since he was admitted, she spent all day, every day at the hospital.

Earlier on the day of November 9th, my mother called to give me an update on Dan's condition as she did every couple of days.

"We had a great day today," she said. "Dan and I, and some of the nurses, watched the Ohio State football game on TV." This year, Ohio State was well on their way to winning the National championship. "They won, of course, and we were all cheering and clapping our hands. Dan was laughing and in a great mood. We even had pizza today," my mother said.

I was exhausted, but still wide awake, when I glanced at the clock on the mantle as it struck midnight. I had just finished watching the last video of the night: *Dragonfly*, starring Kevin Costner. In the movie, Costner's wife dies tragically, and she desperately tries to get a message to him from beyond death by sending various "signs" through near-death, hospitalized children. Costner plays a doctor in the movie. By the end of the movie, Costner finally figures out the message from his dead wife. Since my son, Michael's, death, I had heard from a number of people that, following the death of their loved one, they had received some sort of "sign" from them. This has not happened to me in the four years since Michael's death.

Before going to bed, I walked over to the mantel and picked up a large framed photo of Michael. "I really wish that you'd send me a sign," I said, looking at the picture. "I'd really like to know you're O.K." I kissed his picture and said, "Happy Birthday, Sweetheart. I love you so much."

"I miss you more than I can put into words," I continued. "My heart is broken. It's amazing, but even though my heart is broken, it just keeps right on beating." "Goodnight," I finally wished him. I cried myself to sleep as I had done the past four years on the night before Michael's birthday. This year, falling asleep was twice as hard since I couldn't stop thinking about my conversation with Dan.

Bad News and a Sign
November 10, 2002

It was very early on Sunday morning, when I was awakened by the sound of the telephone ringing. I could not have been asleep more than two hours.

"Who could be calling this early on Sunday morning?" I thought. Today would have been Michael's forty-second birthday.

"Hello?" I said, while yawning. The voice on the other end was one I hadn't heard in over four years. It was Becky calling.

"I'm sorry, Linda," Becky said, "but Dan died last night, a little past midnight. Mom was holding his hand when he died. She's asleep now; the doctor gave her a sedative. She's been up most of the night, in shock and hysterical." My sister continued as if prompted, "I owe you an apology, Linda, for my actions after Michael died. As soon as we hang up, I'm also going to call Sheri and Trisha (*my two daughters*) and apologize to them, too."

I began to cry as I remembered the scenes following Michael's death. Finally I said, "I accept your apology, Bec; I forgive you. Let's not talk about that anymore."

"Why is this happening to us?" I cried in disbelief, "First Dad died; then, nine months later, Omar (*our stepfather*) died. Then, almost nine months later, Michael died. And now Dan! Why?"

"I just spoke with Dan yesterday, and he seemed very upset," I said to Becky. "What happened?"

"The hospital phoned me in Arizona, and said that he started hemorrhaging. They couldn't stop the bleeding. I flew into Columbus early this morning," Becky continued. "Ever since Dan was admitted to the hospital, the doctors haven't been able to treat his leukemia because of the cellulitis infection that he contracted after he entered the hospital."

"So, the fact is," I said, sobbing, "Dan would still be alive if he hadn't gone into the hospital! What a crock! I've always heard hospitals are responsible for killing more patients than anyone could possibly imagine!"

I tried to pull myself together and focus on the practicalities of caring for our grieving mother. "Will you be staying there with Mom?"

"Just for tonight and tomorrow," Becky answered. "Then I have to fly back to Arizona. We have some major problems with NCFE (*Becky's company, National Century Financial Enterprises*) right now that I have to attend to. I'll tell you about it when I see you. When will you be able to come up? Do you think maybe you and Gary, *Becky's bodyguard and friend,* could make all the arrangements for the funeral? I'll pay for everything, and I will keep in close touch by cell phone."

I was not surprised Becky had other, more important things to take care of and that she offered to pay for everything, as usual. This was her standard way of attempting to make up for the fact that she was too busy to be there in person. Unfortunately, this was a pattern the entire family had gotten used to over the years.

"Of course, I can handle the arrangements," I said. "I'll leave early tomorrow morning and should be there by late afternoon. It's about a nine hour drive from here. I'll have to phone my boss, and, since Sheri and Trisha will be coming up later for the funeral, I'll have to find someone to look after the kitties." I ended the conversation by saying, "Tell Mom I love her, and I'll be there tomorrow afternoon."

After we hung up, I suddenly remembered it was Michael's birthday! Dan had died on Michael's birthday, just after midnight!

"Oh, my God!" I gasped. I glanced at Michael's picture on the mantel, and suddenly realized what had happened. Goosebumps covered my entire body. Michael had given me the "sign" I had asked him for a few hours earlier. Dan had died at the exact same time that I begged Michael for a sign.

"Wow!" I thought, "That was no coincidence." Dan and Michael were always very close, like two peas in a pod, always happy, always making everyone laugh.

"Now I know that you're both O.K.," I said aloud, "I'll be all right, too." While glancing at Michael's picture, I said, "Happy Birthday, Michael!"

I learned later my mother was unable to sleep the night of Dan's death. She left the hospital after watching the OSU football game on television with Dan, and arrived at home before dark. My mother was unable to sleep that night; her intuition told her something was wrong with Dan at the hospital. She couldn't see well enough to drive after dark. So, she phoned her younger sister, Clara, and asked if she would drive her to the hospital. Clara worked nights during the week; my mother knew that she would be awake on a Saturday night. They arrived at the hospital around midnight. Dan died just a few minutes past midnight, holding my mother's hand.

A Sad Trip
November 11-15, 2002

I phoned my boss to request a week of unpaid vacation; then I headed north to Columbus for Dan's funeral. I had spent my week of paid vacation – including my birthday – with Dan in his hospital room, just a few weeks earlier. It was difficult for me to take this much time off from my position as Accounting Manager for a large landscape company in Atlanta, Georgia. I managed a staff of five accounting clerks who required lots of supervision. I did not care about that at the moment. All I could think about was that I needed to be in Columbus, with my mother.

I made the drive in record time, and arrived at my mother's house late in the afternoon. She met me at the door, and we hugged as she began crying hysterically. Her eyes were red and swollen. She looked like she had not slept in days. "What am I going to do without him?" she said, tears streaming down her cheeks.

Dan was her pride and joy, her oldest child, and her only son. Becky was the baby, and I was the middle child. Becky was five years younger than I; she got me in trouble with our mother a lot. Dan did, too. When my mother wasn't looking, he would do something to make me scream; then, I would get punished for screaming. As an adult, I was always kidding that I was the "abused" middle child. When we were growing up, I got blamed and punished for everything that went wrong. I remembered how much I hated it when my mother insisted that I forgive Becky every night for all the mean things she had done to me during the day. Becky knew she had done wrong; she was afraid to go to sleep until she was forgiven.

My mother was all alone in the house when I arrived in Columbus. I thought it was strange that Becky had not stayed with her. When I asked about Becky, my mother said, "Something is terribly wrong with Becky's business, and she had to meet with her attorneys."

Since I had not heard from Becky in almost four years before yesterday morning, I had no idea what was happening with her and her company. I didn't really care, either. My relationship with Becky had worsened considerably after she married Don Ayers, her previous husband. Ayers was a very wealthy man, and the entire family saw less and less of Becky after their marriage. When we did get together, once or twice a year, Ayers treated the rest of the family like second-class relatives. Subsequently, we all considered him a huge snob. According to Becky, she divorced him when she discovered that he had been taking a very young girl on trips to Mexico – on their company plane no less.

I spent the remainder of the day consoling my mother and grieving the loss of my big brother, Dan. We reminisced that Dan always made everyone laugh. He had a lust for life, was an avid golfer and had many, many friends. He always joked, "When I go, I'll be ninety-some years old, and I'll get shot by some woman's husband while jumping out of her bedroom window!" I wish it could have happened that way. Sixty-two is much too young to die.

From age seventeen to age thirty-seven, Dan was a sailor in the U.S. Navy, traveling all over the world. We did not see him much during those years, but he always kept in touch, sent letters and gifts for birthdays and holidays. He never forgot. After 20 years, he retired from the Navy and settled in California for a while. He moved to Columbus, Ohio in the early 1980s. From that point on, he became incredibly close to our mother. It was almost like he was trying to make up for all the years he had missed being there for her.

In the past five years, all the men in my immediate family had died. First, my father died; nine months later, my step-father, Omar, died. Then, almost nine months later, my son, Michael, died. I had also recently lost my ex-husband, two uncles and my very best friend, Margaret Johnson. All these losses compounded the grief I was feeling at losing my big brother, Dan.

The next day, Becky called to ask if I could meet her for a late lunch; apparently she was already back in Columbus. It was a rather cool reception after four years. I was fairly certain that, before he died, Dan had asked her to apologize to my daughters and me, just as he had asked me to forgive Becky and take care of our mother.

After some tears and conversation over the death of Dan, Becky handed me an envelope and said, "This is a copy of Dan's Last Will. He left everything he had to you and me. He told Mom he hoped this would bring the two of us closer together."

Looking back, quite the contrary happened. My mother told me later Dan had discussed his Will with her several times just prior to his death. She had told him that she did not want him to leave anything to her. My mother reminded him that Becky had millions of dollars at her disposal, and had promised to take care of her when she needed assistance of any kind. Becky was planning to move our mother into her home, a multi-million dollar ranch in Arizona, when it became necessary. Because of Becky's generous promise, my mother had no life insurance or long-term care insurance. After my mother's husband, Omar, died, my mother even deeded her house in Columbus over to Becky.

Dan had a large metal safe in a closet in his condominium. In the safe, he kept cash, along with his coin collections and valuable proof sets. He gave my mother the combination just before he died, and he told her to remove all the cash and one-ounce gold pieces, approximately forty of them. Dan wanted my mother to have the cash and gold coins for her retirement since she insisted on not being in his Will. After Dan died, my mother gave all the gold coins to Becky. The coins were worth over a thousand dollars each at that time. Later, when I was helping take care of my mother's finances, I saw she had also written a check to Becky for $5,000 at that time. Becky had arrived in Columbus two days before me and had keys to Dan's condo; my mother had given her the combination to Dan's safe. Dan's large collection of valuable proof sets never showed up in the final accounting of his estate. His wheat penny collection – more than 800 rolls of coins – was accounted for in the estate, but the most valuable years were missing.

I was not surprised by my mother's actions, but I was extremely hurt. I had been struggling, financially, to make ends meet, and Becky was a multi-millionaire! It was common family knowledge that Becky was going to take care of my mother in her old age. In response, my mother felt obligated to give Becky everything she had. And she did just that. Becky had a way of making one feel obligated to her if she did something nice for you.

Once again, Becky had to leave town that day to fly to a meeting with her attorneys somewhere. She said she needed to take care of some business for her company, NCFE. She reminded me that Gary would be flying into Columbus to help me make the arrangements for Dan's funeral and cemetery. As usual, she would be in touch by cell phone.

Dan's funeral and burial took place on Wednesday, November 13th.

On Friday, November 15, 2002 – just two days after Dan's funeral – the FBI raided Becky's company, National Century Financial Enterprises, and closed its doors permanently due to fraudulent operations.

Grieving and Confused
November 16 - 23, 2002

My mother was barely functioning and could not understand why Becky was not there with the rest of the family. Except for the funeral and burial, we had not seen Becky all week. Some of the family, myself included, had traveled hundreds of miles to support each other during this sad time. On Saturday, the 16th instead of spending time with my mother and the rest of the family, Becky decided to go to a football game in Indiana with some friends, and from there was heading back to her home in Arizona. I decided to stay another week with my mother. I just could not leave her alone after what she had been through this past week. And, to top it all off, the closing of NCFE was all over the newspapers and television news. As a former CEO and member of the board, Becky's name was always mentioned as one of the founders and one of the suspects in the $2.4 billion company fraud scandal. All this negative publicity really bothered my mother. She was old-fashioned and cared a great deal about what other people thought about her and her family.

The remainder of the second week was spent mostly consoling my mother and going through boxes of documents and pictures from Dan's condo. Becky would not give me the keys to Dan's condo, but gave them to her son, Bobby, and *allowed* me to enter the condo to gather up boxes as long as Bobby was there with me. Most of the papers were of a personal nature, not financial. One significant paper that I found was Dan's original 401k beneficiary statement which named Natasha, his daughter, as primary beneficiary and me as secondary beneficiary. We found out later that while Dan was in the hospital, just days before he died, Becky had him complete the necessary paperwork to close out his 401k, and make her the sole beneficiary! Natasha, a young, single, working mother with two little boys to support, hired an attorney but, in the end, Becky alone ended up with Dan's 401k funds of approximately $50,000.

Dan's Last Will and Testament was also drawn up just days before he died. The attorney who prepared the Will was additionally named the Executor of Dan's estate. His name was Jack Miller.* Mr. Miller was a longtime attorney for NCFE and, at the same time, Becky's personal attorney and extremely close friend for many years. Becky had made sure that she held **all** the cards as far as the distribution of Dan's estate was concerned. Under those circumstances, she would be able to take whatever she wanted, and leave the rest of the family nothing.

***The names of some individuals have been changed. Such names are indicated by an asterisk the first time each appears in the narrative.**

California Dreamin'
November 24 - December 31, 2002

I hated to leave my mother, but I had no choice. I had to go back to my job and family in Georgia. On the 603-mile return trip, I had plenty of time to think about my present situation and my future. Dan was only sixty-two years old, just three years older than me. I loved being near my daughter, Trisha, and her family, but I did not enjoy living in the Atlanta area at all. The traffic was horrible, and everything was so spread out that it took hours to get anywhere. If it rained, forget about it! The backed-up traffic situation was always a nightmare.

My older daughter, Sheri and I talked many times about moving back to California again. We both loved living out there. The problem was that housing was extremely expensive. Everything else seemed relatively inexpensive. Utility costs were low since the climate is so temperate; one rarely needed a heater or air conditioning. A profusion of good, organic food is grown locally, and its proximity makes it much more economical than shipped produce. Back in 1997, I had moved to the Santa Ynez Valley near Santa Barbara after selling my business located in Columbus. My son, Michael, and his family lived in Huntington Beach, and Sheri lived nearby.

After Michael died in 1998, Sheri and I decided to move to Georgia to be near Trisha and her family.

We both felt battered and disillusioned working in downtown Atlanta, however. After five months, we decided to move back to California. This time, we lived in Solvang, a cute little Danish town accented with windmills and bakeries. The entire town is lit up like Christmas all year round. I lived two blocks from the downtown area which included a park with a gazebo in the middle. Sheri lived one block from me. We both loved it there. Sheri and I became best friends as well as mother and daughter over the years. We usually didn't live in the same house, but whenever and wherever I moved, Sheri moved nearby.

Following the nationally tragic events of September 11, 2001, we became homesick for our family back East. So, once again, we moved back to Georgia and were still living there when Dan died.

I kept in close touch with my mother in Ohio for the remainder of 2002. The winter holidays were hard to get through, but my spirits were buoyed by being near Sheri, Trisha, my son-in-law Tom, and my two grandsons, Aaron and Tony. I was still grieving for my son, Michael and missing my four grandchildren in California.

The past four years had been a nightmare filled with losses and grieving. I was convinced things had to get better. I had to get better. I made every effort to think only positive thoughts, and focus on one of my favorite sayings by author Vivian Green, "Life is not about waiting for the storm to pass…it's about learning how to dance in the rain!"

The Lion's Share
2003

B ack in Georgia, in addition to working a full time job, spending time with my family and maintaining close contact with my mother, much of the year was spent in conflict with Becky and Attorney Miller over Dan's estate. Since I lived so far away, it became necessary for me to hire a local Columbus attorney in order to protect my legal interests. The attorney I hired was a nice guy, fairly easygoing, but not very aggressive when it came to dealing with the likes of Becky and her attorney, Mr. Miller. Many of Dan's assets: Rolex watch, wallet, valuable rings, coin proof sets, expensive pool table and a $3,000 disability check never appeared in the distribution list of his assets. I found out later that Becky gave Dan's high-priced pool table to one of her close friends without discussing it with me. Instead of Dan's mail being forwarded to the Executor (the normal procedure), Becky had Dan's mail forwarded to our mother's Columbus address. My mother would then forward the mail to Becky personally in Arizona; she would do whatever Becky asked her to do without question. Since Becky had keys to Dan's condo, car, safe, and more, and since she and Attorney Miller were such close friends, Becky had an inordinate amount of control over the distribution of Dan's assets.

On the estate distribution list, I had asked for Dan's Ping golf putter. Even though it showed up on my half of the distribution list, I never received it. When I asked Becky about it, she told me she put the putter in Dan's casket with him. Thinking that was a sweet gesture, I took Becky at her word, until it showed up in Becky's golf bag. Attorney Miller's final accounting of Dan's total estate amounted to a little more than $100,000, which included the equity in his condo. For services rendered, Attorney Miller charged over $28,000! I filed a grievance with the State of Ohio, Columbus Bar Association, but that turned out to be a total waste of time, and the effort cost me over $500. After all the bills were paid, my distribution was just enough to pay for my Columbus attorney. I was extremely grateful Dan thought of me in his Last Will. It was a true shame his noble intention of bringing Becky and I closer together by bequeathing all his assets to us both, would end up pushing us even further apart.

Becky was always more generous to friends and other family than she was to me. It was obvious to close family and friends, especially my children, that Becky never outgrew the sibling rivalry between us. She was always extremely jealous of my close relationship with my son, Michael, and my two daughters. Her own son, Bobby, was virtually raised by our mother since Becky worked all of the time and was out of town incessantly.

Becky was also jealous of the fact I graduated from college, specifically Ohio State University. She was conspicuously absent at my graduation even though I was the *first* and *only* member of our family to *ever* graduate from college. It took me more than seven years to earn my BS Degree in Accounting from OSU because I was a single mother with two teenage daughters still in school, and I worked full time as an accountant at Nationwide Insurance. Graduation day was one of the most beautiful compensations of my life. The entire family attended the graduation ceremony and celebration, all except Becky.

Becky never attended OSU, or any college. She had the means financially, so instead of earning a degree, she bought memberships in the OSU President's Club. She bought season tickets to OSU football games and hobnobbed with OSU football coaches, players and faculty. To my great sadness, she never invited me to any special events at my own alma mater.

Spark of a Dream
April 1, 2003

On April Fool's Day, 2003, Sheri married Albert Contreras, a young man originally from the town of La Tinaja, in the state of Veracruz, Mexico. I told an old friend I might be living in Veracruz some day because Sheri offered to take care of me in my old age. He laughed when I told him what she had specifically said: "I promise I will change your dirty diapers when you get old!" She's a very special daughter, and, after she married Albert, we talked often about the possibility of living in Veracruz someday.

Surprise Subpoena
May 7, 2003

O n May 7, at approximately 9:00 p.m., I pulled into my garage upon returning from a shopping trip. It was pouring rain, and my garage door was still open, when an unfamiliar man in a business suit walked up to me and said, "Are you Linda Case?"

"Yes, what do you want?"

While handing me his business card, he said, "My name is Michael Davis.* I'm a Special Agent from the Columbus Federal Bureau of Investigation, and I'd like to speak to you regarding your sister, Rebecca."

"I have nothing to say," I replied, "I don't know anything about NCFE and, before my brother's funeral a few months ago, I had not spoken to Becky in four years. I'm really sorry, but I have nothing to say."

At that point, he handed me an envelope which contained a subpoena, ordering me to appear before a federal grand jury in Columbus on June 3, 2003, at 9:00 a.m. The subpoena also commanded me to bring a very long list of "any financial records, open or closed, held for or in the name of Rebecca Parrett." Since I knew nothing about Becky's financial matters, let alone NCFE's, and since I had already used all my vacation time from work, including one week *without* pay, I really did not want to do this. I hired an attorney from a large, well-known legal firm in Columbus. Three attorneys from the firm were former tax clients of mine, now retired. One of them referred me to a lawyer from the same firm who specialized in criminal law. After lots of paperwork and a $500 attorney fee, I was excused from appearing in person before the federal grand jury.

The remainder of 2003 passed without any further contact with Becky.

State of Mind
2004

Several times a week I telephoned my mother in Ohio. Her health was constantly on my mind since neither Dan nor Becky were around to look after her. I also frequently called my Aunt Clara, who lived near my mother. My mother, Nellie, was the oldest of nine children, and Clara was the youngest. Because of the twenty year age difference, Nellie was more like a mother than a sister to Clara. They were very close, especially after Clara moved to Columbus approximately twenty years ago. Often, my mother would tell me, "Clara calls me every day, just to check to see if I'm all right. She's really good to me." Unfortunately, despite Clara checking on her regularly, my mother's health continued to decline.

The newspapers were full of the National Century scandal, and my mother sounded more depressed each time we spoke. Being old-fashioned, she was intensely concerned about friends and neighbors opinions regarding her and her family's reputation. My mother was extremely embarrassed her daughter, Becky, was involved in such a scandalous crime, especially since she had bragged about Becky for so many years. My mother would phone me crying, each time an article would appear in the morning paper or she heard about it on the local television news. She became especially upset when Becky's name was mentioned or, even worse, when a picture of Becky appeared, which happened frequently. I felt so helpless, being so very far away, in Georgia.

It was spring in Georgia, and, for several months, Sheri and I were formulating our plans to move back to the Santa Barbara area of California. We decided to head west in May since our route to Santa Barbara involved going over some high elevations and possibly bad weather. I could not wait to return to California, where the weather was almost perfect! I have often heard when a city lies between the mountains and the ocean, as Santa Barbara does, this creates *happiness.* A quote written by Bill Zeldis from a Santa Barbara-themed calendar puts it eloquently:

"It's often said that Santa Barbara is a state of mind, but it is definitely a place as well, where even the simple things have a peculiar majesty. A windy beach, a knife-edged horizon, a few gulls bobbing on the water; they all have a certain clarity that seems, if not unique, at least native to this place."

Indeed, Santa Barbara and the Santa Ynez Valley are breathtakingly beautiful. When I first moved to the Valley back in 1997, I kept a camera in my car and took hundreds of photographs of rainbows, sunsets and the countryside. This was paradise, and I felt it was exactly where I was meant to live. I was so very happy! Less than a year after I moved to California, my son died suddenly, and my happiness seemed to evaporate.

"Happiness is like a butterfly which appears and delights us for one brief moment, but soon flits away," said Anna Pavlova as quoted in *Meditations for Women Who Do Too Much* by Anne Wilson Schaef.

Schaef also wrote in her book, "There is no difference between happiness and depression. They both have the same process. It is just the content that is not the same. Both will come and go. The major difference between them is what we *do* with them. We are always seeking happiness. When we see it coming we say, 'Ah, come here, I see you. Stay with me always.' Happiness laughs and says, 'Oh, she's seen me, I can leave now.' And it does. With depression, we see it coming, and we say: 'Go away, I don't want you. Not me.' And depression sighs and says, 'Here we go again, I'm going to have to get bigger and bigger for her to hear me and learn what I have to teach.' So it taps us on the shoulder and says, 'Over here, over here!' until it gets our attention. Then it leaves."

Five long years had gone by since I left the Santa Ynez Valley after my son Michael's death. It was now time for me to return to California. I missed my son's children. I missed the peacefulness and breathtaking landscape of the Valley and Santa Barbara, where the mountains and ocean meet the rainbows and the sunsets. I was happy there. I knew I could find happiness again in spite of everything that had happened in Ohio.

A Big Birthday
May 14, 2004

Sheri and Albert began searching for jobs in California via the internet, while I planned a side trip to Columbus to visit my mother for her eightieth birthday on May 14th. Sheri set up some job interviews in California for the same week that I was going to be in Columbus. She wasn't able to accompany me.

When I arrived at my mother's, I couldn't believe my eyes. She had lost a tremendous amount of weight; she was a nervous wreck, and her eyes were like two black holes from a lack of sleep. We hugged one another and cried together for a long, long time. It broke my heart to see my mother so deeply depressed and in such frail physical health.

My mother's sister, Goldie, and Goldie's husband, Cecil, came to Columbus from Florida to celebrate the milestone birthday. Cecil's birthday was May 15th; so they decided to celebrate their eightieth birthdays together. Goldie was the second oldest of the nine siblings. Naturally, my mother and she had always been very close. Cecil had always teased my mother that he was younger than she was – by minutes; he had always been able to make her laugh. Aunt Goldie told me later she was really concerned about my mother's weight loss and her overall appearance. She said she just couldn't imagine how my mother was coping with the loss of her beloved Dan.

I played hostess, chauffeur, cook, dish washer, and nurse during that week. We visited relatives we had not seen in ages and had a huge family birthday dinner, laughing and crying together. My mother had a good week. Many of her friends, and most of the family, came to visit at different points during the week. There was one very noticeable absence, Becky. Once again, Becky's priorities precluded her presence at a special family occasion. I could see the pain on my mother's face whenever anyone asked, "Where's Becky?"

When the time came for me to return to Georgia, my mother began to cry again. My heart ached for her. How could I move to California now? On the drive back to Georgia, 603 miles, I cried the whole way, realizing I would have to put my dreams on hold to care for my mother. Almost two years had passed since the National Century scandal began; I was fairly certain that the trial would be starting soon. Once the trial was over, I hoped the media frenzy would end, and my mother would regain her health. At that point, I could resume my plans to move to California. As soon as I got home, I phoned my daughters.

"Mom really needs me right now, Sheri. So, as soon as possible, I'll be moving to Columbus, at least until Becky's trial is over. With Dan gone, if Becky is convicted, I'm afraid it will kill her."

Dreams on Hold
July 31, 2004

S heri and I made a trip to Columbus over the July 4th holiday to search for housing for each of us. Sheri had also decided to move to Ohio temporarily, to support me in caretaking my mother, her grandmother. We were fortunate to find two condominiums to rent a few yards from each other in the Hidden Lake area. The neighborhood was less than two miles away from my mother's house. It was very important for me to be nearby.

My mother hadn't changed much since May; she was still crying all the time. Her face lit up like a Christmas tree when we told her we were both moving back to Columbus. On July 31, 2004, Sheri and Albert, my three cats and I moved into our respective condos at Hidden Lake.

If Becky was convicted in the NCFE fraud case, my mother would not only be devastated but would also be forced to move out of her home where she had lived for many years. Soon after Omar, my stepfather, died in 1997, Becky convinced my mother to deed their house over to her. Remember, Becky had promised to take care of my mother in her old age. If Becky was convicted however, the government would seize all of Becky's assets, including my mother's house. My mother would not have Becky's financial help **or** her own house to live in if that happened. In that regrettable eventuality, I was planning to move my mother into an apartment close to her sister, Clara. When that time arrived, if my mother was not physically and mentally healthy, and able to care for herself, I would have to make other arrangements. For my mother's sake, I was praying Becky would be found innocent.

My sole reason for moving to Columbus was to look after my mother, to be there for her when Becky's verdict was decided. I wanted to spend most of my time helping my mother, but it was financially necessary for me to find a job right away. As soon as tax season 2005 arrived, I was confident I would be able to find a position preparing income tax returns. For almost thirty years, from January through April each year, I had done just that. Many of those years I was the sole owner of Case Accounting and Tax Service, located in Columbus. Although I received a Bachelor of Science in Accounting from Ohio State University, my love was the preparation of individual income tax returns. Each return was a new challenge! After years of preparing over four hundred tax returns each year, I became an expert. My clients called me "Linda Loophole."

January was still six months away, however. In a declining economy, at age 61, I felt fortunate to find a part-time bookkeeping position with a family-owned commercial painting company. The location was perfect, very close to my mother's house and my condo.

I did not see or speak to Becky during the entire year of 2004.

Sidelined, Again
2005

As I had hoped, I obtained a position with a CPA firm in Worthington Ohio preparing income tax returns full time from January through April. Those four months went by like a blur since I was still working part-time at the painting company and spending more time with my mother. I needed the money, as our plans had adapted slightly due to the circumstances. Sheri, Albert and I were looking for a house to buy together, one that would be big enough for the three of us, as well as my mother, in the very near future.

My mother was beginning to do weird things. One day, she phoned me crying. I rushed right over to find her sitting in her car, in the alley, near her home. She had an appointment with her family doctor for her six-month check-up and couldn't remember how to get there. I drove her that day and to all future doctor appointments. I was glad because it gave me a chance to discuss my mother's health, privately, with her doctor. He recommended that I make an appointment for her with a neurologist, but she absolutely refused.

Over the past two years, since Dannie's death in 2002, my mother had been on medications for depression and nerves and had been losing weight. After that day, my mother got lost many times while driving around town. Some of the incidents she would mention to me, but I was certain there were many more she didn't tell me about. She told her sister, Clara, "If

Linda knew how often I got lost, she would really be upset." About this same time, my mother began repeating herself quite frequently.

Another incident, which I remember very vividly, was the day she called, and asked me to come help her find her teeth! When I arrived, I found her with a butcher knife in her hand, standing next to an expensive upholstered chair which she had completely demolished. She said she was certain her teeth had fallen out and were "somewhere inside the chair". After several more hours of searching, we found them underneath her pillow in her bedroom, far from the accused chair!

In June, Becky phoned from Arizona to say she was leaving the next day for Managua, Nicaragua, supposedly on some sort of mission with her church. She said she was taking out a million dollar insurance policy on herself, and she wanted to make me one of the beneficiaries. She asked for my social security number, and I gave it to her, never giving it a second thought. When I told my daughter, Sheri what I did, she said, "Mom, you are so naïve. You should know that Becky's not going to make you the beneficiary of anything! It's hard to tell what she will do with your social security number! You'd better call that U.S. Marshal, the one that brought the subpoena to Georgia after Dan died, and tell him what happened." As soon as we hung up, I searched for the marshal's business card and phoned him immediately. He was very pleased that I gave him this information.

The next time I spoke with Becky was in mid-July, just prior to the annual Dannie Mayes Memorial Golf Outing. After I moved to Columbus, my mother told me about the annual outings and was shocked Becky hadn't mentioned them to me before. I wasn't surprised. I rarely heard from Becky unless she wanted something from me, like the social security incident. The outing had been an annual event for two years, since Dan's death. Dan loved golf and used to play several times a week, mostly with his friends from the Rendezvous Lounge in Dublin, Ohio. Dan was treasurer of the Rendezvous Golf League for many years, and he was active in several other golf leagues in the Dublin area.

After Dan's death, Rendezvous owners and close friends organized the annual fundraiser in memory of Dan. The proceeds were donated to the Ohio State University James Cancer Hospital, where Dan spent the last weeks of his life. Each year, the outing raised thousands of dollars which were donated to the hospital in Dan's memory. Dan had many friends who loved him very much.

I had never been invited to the annual golf outings while living in Georgia. In fact, I never even knew they existed until now. Truthfully, I probably wouldn't have driven the six hundred to attend, but as Dan's sister, it would have been nice to have been invited, at least. My mother and Aunt Clara had always attended the outings as guests. I enjoyed golf; a few years prior, I played in three different leagues every week. For my mother's sake, I attended the 2005 Memorial Golf Outing. I even volunteered to be the scorekeeper. While the golfers were out golfing, my mother, Clara and I had a great time enjoying the refreshments and chatting with everyone. Becky and Gary played golf that day in a foursome with two of Becky's closest friends.

Becky and I spoke only briefly throughout the entire day. In fact, Becky did not even mention she and Gary were planning a huge wedding, occurring in just a few weeks. I was shocked when I later heard the news from my mother. Just a few months earlier in March, I had received an e-mail from Becky stating "Gary went back to California to be with his kids. We're still friends, but the personal side of our relationship was never going to be more than friends."

On August 27, 2005, Becky and Gary were married at the Crystal Cathedral Chapel in California by the Rev. Robert Schuller. Becky was a fan and close friend of Rev. Schuller, who according to Becky, frequently accompanied her to various events throughout the country via National Century's company jet.

I did not receive an invitation, but was not surprised at the snub. My daughters, Sheri and Trisha, were also not invited. I was surprised, however, that both my granddaughters, Michael's daughters, Honey and Marlee, were not only invited but were actual *participants* in the ceremony! My daughter-in-law, Cora also attended with her new husband, Bruce. Before Michael died, Becky would frequently treat my son and his family to expensive outings, like tickets to the Super Bowl, lunches at the Ritz, without inviting me. When I mentioned her upcoming nuptials to Becky, she said it was "not going to be a big wedding". According to my mother, Becky's dress alone cost $15,000! After the wedding, a lavish reception was held on a yacht with hundreds of guests attending. Then, the newlyweds spent a two week honeymoon in Costa Rica.

In November, after many months of searching for just the right house, Sheri, Albert and I moved into our new house in Grove City, Ohio, a suburb of Columbus.

Indictment in the News
May - June 2006

It was a new year. I spent income tax season working for the same CPA firm in Worthington and, once again, those four months flew by in a blur. I really loved the challenge of preparing income tax returns and always felt that it was the perfect occupation to have if you lived in Ohio. By the time tax season was over, the cold, grey days had disappeared and spring had arrived. Although I worked many long hours January through April, the rest of the year was spent just being together with my mother. That was the whole idea behind my move to Ohio. Almost two years had passed since I moved to Ohio to await Becky's trial and over three years had passed since the closure of Becky's company. The trial date had been scheduled several times but was always cancelled and rescheduled for various reasons.

In May, life began to slow down a bit. Sheri, Albert and I celebrated with my mother on her eighty-second birthday. I had not seen or spoken to Becky since we exchanged a few words the past Christmas.

On May 22, 2006, Becky was indicted. The indictment was forty-nine pages long; it charged Becky with thirty-six counts, including conspiracy, money laundering conspiracy, promoting money laundering, securities fraud, wire fraud, and mail fraud. Becky and six other former executives of the defunct National

Century Financial Enterprises were indicted for their roles in engineering a $3 billion fraud at their health-care financing company. Their arraignment was held on June 2, 2006, wherein all seven pleaded "not guilty."

During the weeks and months following the indictment, pictures of Becky appeared on the front page of *The Columbus Dispatch* and all three local TV news programs. Articles also appeared in the *Wall Street Journal, Business News Journal, U.S. News Journals* and newspapers, journals and magazines all across the country. Pictures of Becky and allegations appeared almost daily. My mother was an avid, daily reader of *The Columbus Dispatch* newspaper and a faithful consumer of the morning, noon and evening local TV news shows. She phoned me, sobbing wildly, every time she read an article in the newspaper or saw Becky's picture on the news.

As previously stated, my mother was old-fashioned; she worried about what others thought of her and members of her family. Her depression and anxiety both increased exponentially during this time and so did her medications. She had bragged about Becky's achievements for so many years, and now she said she was "really embarrassed" when friends and family began to contact her in curiosity and concern. My mother had never really grasped the severity of the 2002 NCFE scandal until now.

An article in *The Arizona Republic,* May 24, 2006 12:00 AM reported:

NORTHEAST VALLEY- A woman who was a top executive in a national health care financing company has been indicted with six others in a multibillion-dollar securities scheme.

Rebecca Parrett, former vice chairwoman and co-owner of National Century Financial Enterprises, was indicted Friday in U.S. District Court in Columbus, Ohio. The indictment alleges she was responsible for providing instructions on moving funds into and out of accounts and preparing reports that falsely represented the company's financial condition.

She is charged with conspiracy, securities fraud, mail fraud, wire fraud and money laundering. The counts carry penalties of five to 20 years in prison and fines of $250,000 to $500,000. Parrett, who was last reported to live in Carefree, could not be reached for comment.

NCFE was based in Dublin, Ohio, with a branch office in Scottsdale. It bought accounts receivable from health care providers around the country, financing the purchases by selling notes to large institutional investors. The indictment alleges that Parrett and other executives diverted funds to other companies they owned, then moved money between accounts and created fake reports to cover up the scheme. The company collapsed in bankruptcy in 2002. Investors worldwide lost an estimated $3 billion. They included the state of Arizona, which had invested $131 million on behalf of the state and various Valley cities and school districts. 'This is a classic case of corrupt corporate insiders creating false accounting records to hide their dishonest actions from investors,' Chip Burrus, acting assistant director of the FBI's criminal investigative division, said in a statement.

Arizona was the only state to invest in National Century. The state lost $38 million in state funds and

$93 million invested by the state treasurer for cities and school districts. The Arizona state treasury officials invested a total of $131 million in NCFE during 2001 and 2002. They received $1 million back from NCFE's bankruptcy, which didn't make them happy. No wonder Becky began spending more time in Ohio. The climate for her in Arizona couldn't be all that friendly, now that she had been criminally indicted. In addition to the main office in Dublin, Ohio, NCFE maintained offices in four other states including North Carolina, Florida, New York and Arizona.

Housing Crunch
June - December

It had already been more than three-and-a-half years since National Century was raided and closed down. Now, finally, I was hopeful the trial would begin. If Becky's verdict was not good, I would be nearby for my mother as planned.

In late June, Becky and Gary made a visit to Columbus. They stayed at my mother's house for more than a week. My mother would always get very nervous and upset when Becky, with or without Gary, would stay at her house. At her age, she just did not like change of any kind. Plus, the house was very small, with only one bathroom, but my mother could never say no to Becky. She would wear herself out, spending every moment of her time trying to make Becky comfortable. After all, she still believed Becky was going to take care of her when she could no longer care for herself. When she stayed there, Becky would always use our mother's car and stay out late which caused my mother to lose sleep and worry.

Becky began coming to Columbus at least once a month to meet with her attorneys. After one of her visits in July, my mother phoned me, in tears. "Becky is going to remodel my house and make herself an office in the basement! She'll be coming into town more frequently until after the trial is over. What am I going to do? I don't want her to do this! I don't want all that noise and dust! What about my cats?"

I wanted to say, "Why didn't you tell this to Becky, Mom?" Sadly, I knew the answer; she was afraid. She did not want to upset Becky. She *never* wanted to do anything that might upset Becky. The next day I called Becky, and, as usual, got her voicemail. I left her a voice message stating all the reasons she should reconsider before remodeling our mother's house. Becky's reply message sounded as if it came from the devil himself. "How dare you tell me what I can or can't do to that house! You GO TO HELL! I OWN that house, and I'll do whatever I please with it! Don't EVER leave me a message like that again!" Then she hung up.

She left me a voice message the next day wherein she apologized, saying, "That was not a very Christian thing to do." Over the past few years, especially after NCFE was raided and closed down, Becky had become intensely involved with a large church in Arizona. She called herself a Christian. According to my mother, Becky had become really good friends with the famous television pastor, Robert Schuller. She spent lots of time with Pastor Schuller at the Crystal Cathedral in California. On occasion, he would accompany Becky on trips aboard the NCFE company plane.

After the "remodeling of Mom's house" incident, I offered Becky a bedroom in my house in Grove City where she could stay when she was in town. She accepted. Previously when in Columbus, Becky had stayed in a room at a friend's house when she was not at our mother's home. I wasn't sure *why* that room was no longer available to her, but I knew my offer to Becky would ease my mother's mind and bring her joy.

It made her so happy when she thought her two girls were getting along. Becky and I both tried to live peaceably and be cordial to one another when my mother was present.

In September, Becky moved some bedroom furniture and clothing into the house in Grove City. The bedroom was large with a private bathroom and a large walk-in closet that I shared. This bedroom had previously belonged to Sheri and Albert; thinking the trial would soon be over, they decided to move ahead to California.

The rest of the year, I saw Becky about once a month. She leased a new 2006 Chrysler PT Cruiser in my mother's name that she kept in my three-car garage. Whenever she'd come into town, I would pick her up at the airport and return her to the airport using the Chrysler. This was about the only time we actually had a chance to talk. She would always leave the house early each day and return after I had already gone to bed.

On October 31, 2006, once again my mother phoned in hysterics! Sobbing and choking so badly I could hardly understand her, she said, "Two men in business suits just came to the door and handed me some papers that I don't understand! They said it was a *lien* against my house!"

"Calm down, Mom," I reassured her, "I'll be right over." She was so upset, I was afraid she would have a stroke or heart attack before I could get there. I got in my car and broke speeding limits to get to her. It was about a twenty minute drive to her house from Grove City. When I arrived, she was shaking and still crying. So, I gave her one of her nerve pills to calm her down.

She picked up a manila envelope from the kitchen table and handed it to me. It had been hand-delivered to my mother personally and stamped "Certified." The first page was a letter addressed to my mother and signed by Dale Williams, Assistant United States Attorney. The letter stated, in part, "Enclosed please find a file-stamped copy of the Plaintiff United States of America's Notice of Lis Pendens with regard to the property located at 2813 Elliott Avenue, Columbus, Ohio." Attached to the letter was the NOTICE OF LIS PENDENS, the actual *lien* against the property. It gave a legal description of the property and stated, basically, that the real property was to be forfeited. I understood now why my mother was so upset. She had forgotten that she deeded her house over to Becky. At some point, my mother would surely be forced to move from her home.

"Well," I thought to myself, "This is the reason I moved to Ohio – to be here when that happened." I didn't let on to my mother, but I was very angry with Becky for talking my mother into signing over her house to Becky. It was that old control issue with Becky. She did it because she could. I felt so very sorry for my mother. She had been through so much over the past few years, and it just seemed to never let up. Now, on top of everything else, she had to worry about losing her home! I fibbed and said, "Mom, this is all just a mistake. Becky has not even been convicted, yet. So, don't worry."

She did worry, however, all the time. Every time an unfamiliar car drove down the alley next to her house, she phoned me to say she was "certain that it was the government, and *they* were going to put her, and her cats, out on the street!" She even wrote me a letter, begging me to call Becky for counsel on this matter. Her letter asked, "Can someone evict me from this? And if so how long do I have? It is worrying me to death. I can hardly sleep, and I am a nervous wreck."

My mother's house was completely paid off several years before my stepfather died in 1997. Now, there was a lien on the property. The house was currently in Becky's name. If she was convicted, my mother's house would become the property of the United States government! There seemed to be nothing we could do.

There was a verbal agreement between my mother and Becky. My mother deeded her house over to Becky and, in exchange, Becky would take care of her for the remainder of her life. The entire immediate family was aware of this arrangement. Dan and I never concerned ourselves as to whether our mother had life insurance or long-term care insurance because Becky was her insurance policy. Even though the agreement was not written and signed, I was under the impression that the verbal agreement was just as binding. I hoped Becky, faced with a possible conviction and prison, had arranged for some sort of protection for our mother's future. If Becky had not arranged something by now, it would be too late, according to Becky's indictment.

Not Very Merry
December 2006

My daughter, Trisha in Georgia phoned me on December 17 with more bad news. My seventeen-year-old grandson, Aaron, had run away from home. She said Aaron was failing in school, got into drugs, and most recently, was sexually involved with a thirteen-year-old girl. There had been a rather heated argument between her, Aaron and Tom, Aaron's stepfather. Now, Aaron had been missing for almost two days!

Trisha seemed very distraught; she offered to purchase a round-trip airline ticket for me if I would come down to Georgia. Maybe I could help, somehow. Aaron and I had always been close. He was a great kid, and I wondered what had gone so terribly wrong. I wanted to be there for Trish, too. My son, Michael, had run away once, so I knew what she must be feeling.

Trish and Tom worked hard to make that Christmas as merry as possible under the circumstances, especially for my other grandson, Tony, who was only eight years old. I hated being away from my mother over the holidays; she told me later it was the worst Christmas she had ever had. Mine was not the greatest, either, although I was grateful to be with Trish and family. For years, my house was the place where the entire family gathered for the Christmas and New Year holidays. I missed those days. This was the first time in my life that I hadn't put up a Christmas tree. I promised myself that it would also be the last. We thought Aaron might come home on Christmas Day, but that did not happen.

The day after Christmas Trish received a phone call – just minutes after dropping me off at the Atlanta airport, Aaron was spotted at a local movie theater. Trish picked him up, and he was back at home in Georgia before my plane landed in Columbus.

A few days later, Trish called me again. She said after several hours of discussions, Aaron was adamant he could no longer live at home; he would simply run away again at the first opportunity. Trisha was ready to enroll him in a locked-down military school. His only other option was to come to Ohio and live with me. Even though my hands were full taking care of my mother, dealing with Becky at my house once or twice a month, and income tax season fast approaching, I just couldn't say no – I loved Aaron too much. I was hopeful Aaron's biological father, Scott, who also lived in Columbus, might be a help in this situation. Sadly, Scott had always been a disappointment as a father to Aaron. We thought he might rise to the occasion if Aaron was living right here in Columbus, but unfortunately, he did not.

Taking Care of Family
2007

On January 11, 2007, Aaron moved into the big house in Grove City. Most of my friends and family said I must be out of my mind to take on the responsibility for a teenager at my age, especially since I was also the caretaker for my mother.

I actually enjoyed having a teenager in the house again. It made me feel younger being a parent again at age 63. At first, we spent lots of time together decorating his bedroom, talking (him talking, me listening) and having pizza at our favorite hangout, Planks on Broadway. Aaron began the last half of his junior year at Grove City High School. He joined the Choir, the ROTC program, played rugby after school and made the Honor roll almost every semester. He was doing great, and I was really proud of him.

It seemed to me he had just been mingling with the wrong crowd in Georgia and needed a change of environment. Seventeen seems to be a tough age for the boys in our family. My son, Michael, got into trouble smoking pot at that age. My brother, Dan ran away from home when he was seventeen and was gone for more than two months.

Soon after Aaron moved in, Becky called and asked me to have a lock put on our shared walk-in closet in her bedroom. She said, "There's a gun in the closet, and I'm afraid Aaron might snoop around and find it." Becky said she had been threatened several times and was afraid for her life. The lives of her son and grandchildren had also been threatened, she said. I knew she slept with a gun under her pillow. According to her, she had filed a lawsuit against "a dirty attorney" from California who cheated her out of approximately $3 million.

She also asked me to purchase a pre-paid, disposable, satellite phone and give her the phone number. She said, "If anything ever happens to me, I will call you on that number. Gary will have one, too, and I will make sure you have his number." So, I did as she asked, I bought the phone and had the lock put on the closet door. From that day forward, the closet was locked at all times. Becky and I each had a key. Becky told me later she dropped her lawsuit against the attorney out of fear for her life as well as that of her son and grandchildren.

For the past several years, I had been driving my mother to her doctor appointments at least once every month. During the last visit, her family doctor had become adamant that she see a neurologist right away. Once again, she absolutely refused. After several months of coaxing and convincing her the appointment was merely for taking some tests, she finally agreed reluctantly. Her first appointment with the neurologist was on February 2. The results of many tests, mostly brain/memory related, indicated that my mother was in the early stages of Alzheimer's disease. The doctor prescribed specific medication for her memory. He said to me, privately, "There is no current cure for Alzheimer's, but the medication will, hopefully, slow the progression. Alzheimer's affects each patient differently."

I was devastated! Her memory would continue to decline, the doctor said. There would be no way she would be able to live independently much longer. I could not imagine how I would cope with her care at that point. Hopefully, Becky would be acquitted and would employ loving, professional care for our mother as it became needed, just as she had always promised.

Sheri was living in California now, employed as an accountant at the Fess Parker Winery in Solvang. I missed her immensely and longed to be back in California again. Now that I was the caretaker for both my mother and Aaron, the dream of moving to California seemed to drift further and further away from reality for me. I've always been a positive person and have always believed that everything happens for a reason. There are no accidents. I told myself I was here in Columbus for a reason.

The month of March was filled with sickness, doctors and hospital visits. My mother had a terrible cold for a couple of weeks which included strep throat. In addition, the neurologist scheduled her for several exploratory surgeries, an MRA and another appointment. Aaron had pneumonia, and he ended up in the emergency room. Not to be left out, while I was cooking Sunday dinner, my nose began bleeding for absolutely no reason; it just would not stop, not even for the emergency medics. So, the medics whisked me off to the closest Urgent Care Center where the doctor finally got my nosebleed under control. After three follow-up visits with Ear, Nose and Throat Specialists, they still couldn't tell me what caused such a nosebleed. I was incredibly relieved when spring arrived, glad to have survived another cold, grey winter in Columbus, Ohio.

For the next few months, my mother and Aaron kept me hopping. My mother occupied me with numerous family doctor appointments, mammograms, bone density tests, and appointments with her neurologist. She was still losing a lot of weight; I think she was forgetting to eat. Aaron was simply a teenage boy adjusting to a new home, new parent, and new high school.

Every six weeks, except when he had pneumonia, Aaron's grades made the honor roll. He became a very popular student at Grove City High. I attended all of his choir concerts, open houses at school, ROTC spaghetti dinners and helped prepare him for his first prom. We also spent a lot of time together filling out forms for various colleges, scholarships and financial aid. I was doing my best to steer him towards my alma mater, Ohio State. He made me very proud to be his grandmother. With honor roll grades, he passed his junior year of high school. In less than six months, he became one of the most popular students in his class.

As a reward for Aaron, and a respite for me, Sheri invited Aaron to spend almost the entire month of June with her and Albert in California. Two of his best friends were invited too, as long as they could pay for their own round-trip transportation. Along with everything else on his plate, Aaron had been working and saving money for "his last summer before graduating and going out into the real world" as he put it. "Aunt Sheri," he said, "gave us the best time of our lives."

On July 2, 2007, my mother phoned me several times. She was upset again and crying. Becky called her to say she was bringing a truckload of Becky's son, Bobby's furniture to store in her house. Becky just did not get it! Once again, I persuaded Becky to use my house instead of our mother's. The furniture and boxes filled one entire garage space, top to bottom. That much stuff would have filled the entire basement of my mother's house, and she would have been very unhappy. Bobby had recently moved back to Columbus from Arizona, but he didn't stay long. After a few months, he moved back to Arizona.

Bobby was an only child; he was spoiled and never really grew up. Becky had always taken care of him, financially, so he never had to work, either. The family lovingly called him a "Professional Son." That was his job. He had been married several times and had two children.

September began my favorite time of the year in Ohio: autumn and Ohio State football. The fall colors were magnificent this year. Once again, Aunt Clara, Aunt Pat and I took my mother for our annual drive through Hocking Hills to view the beautiful scenery, especially along Skyline Drive in southern Ohio. We always stopped for lunch and delicious home-made pies at the Old Towne Restaurant in Laurelville. We made it a tradition to visit several gift shops along the trail and would never pass up the Farmers' Market where we purchased apples for Thanksgiving pies and enjoyed a cup of fresh apple cider.

Life was passing by so quickly. Aaron was now in his senior year at Grove City High School. I decided to show him what college *tradition* was all about by taking him to an Ohio State football game, complete with pre-game brunch at the Blackwell Center, close to the stadium. I wanted Aaron to experience the tradition of Ohio State football and TBDBITL, The Best Damn Band in the Land at "The Shoe," otherwise known as Ohio Stadium. I've been to many other college football games, but I have never experienced another school that celebrates tradition like Ohio State University. I am still moved to tears and goose bumps every time the band and drum major march onto the field, playing "Carmen Ohio" and forming "Script Ohio". I earnestly wanted to share that deeply moving experience with my grandson to inspire him. We spent a memorable day together.

On November 2nd, Aaron turned eighteen. We had a huge Halloween/Birthday party complete with costumes, pumpkin carving contest and a menu to "die" for: scary homemade chili, deviled eggs, spookie barbecue, witches brew, black cat cake and ice cream. We were having so much fun together. Aaron brought joy back into my life.

Becky was spending more and more of her time in Ohio. Up to now, the trial had been scheduled to begin several different times but was always postponed and rescheduled. It had been scheduled for November, but once again, was postponed. The new trial date was scheduled for February 3, 2008. It had now been over five years since NCFE was raided and closed by the FBI. Becky was assured by her lawyers the trial would not be postponed this time.

Since February would be the dead-of-winter and Becky would be spending a lot more time with her attorneys and at the courthouse, she decided to rent an apartment downtown within walking distance of the courthouse. The first week in December, Gary came to Columbus and moved Becky into the apartment. Beginning in January, 2008, she planned to stay in Columbus full time, until the trial ended.

Meanwhile, my mother was beginning to get lost more frequently, even going to the grocery store which was just a few blocks away. She would never admit it to me, but she would often tell her sister, Clara, who would share the information with me. My mother continued to do other little things that concerned me, too. For instance, one month when paying her bills, she paid an $800 gas bill in error. In December 2007, she sent not one but three Christmas cards to each of her friends and family, me included. She also continued to lose weight; I think she was hesitant to cook because she was afraid of setting the house on fire. If confronted about her diet, she would say, "I eat a lot of peanut butter and jelly sandwiches, which I love."

A Shred of Hope
February 3, 2008

Finally! More than five years had passed since this nightmare began for our family. Since the trial was at last starting, it would soon be over. Aaron would graduate in May, and I would have my life back! For my mother's sake, I was praying that Becky would be found innocent.

Once again the newspapers and television media were full of Becky's picture and lots of derogatory comments. In the article, "Trial in Huge Fraud Case to Begin," published February 3, 2008 on the front page of *The Columbus Dispatch* reported:

As fraud cases go, the National Century Financial Enterprises case ranks up there with Enron and WorldCom, prosecutors say. Investors in the Dublin-based company lost more than $1.9 billion after the financing giant filed for bankruptcy in 2002. And at least 275 health-care companies collapsed, putting thousands out of work and affecting thousands of patients. National Century's collapse never gained much attention outside business circles, largely because it was a privately held company. But some, such as large pension funds and the state of Arizona, lost millions. 'I always say it's the largest, most significant case you've never heard of,' said Kathy Patrick, an Arizona attorney representing 30 clients who lost a total of $1.6 billion.

Guilty, Guilty, Guilty
February 4 - March 13, 2008

A rticles began appearing in newspapers and on television news shows almost daily. My mother was getting really nervous and depressed again. She was terrified of losing her home and her daughter. She cried a lot, too. I tried to talk her into coming to live with me, but my mother has always been extremely stubborn and independent. Last September, there was a terrible storm and her electricity was off for an entire week. She still insisted on staying in her house. Aunt Clara was a tremendous help to me when dealing with my mother. She and I regularly compared notes and discussed how scared we were for my mother's safety.

I did not follow the trial apart from an occasional television news broadcast. It was the busiest time of the year for my small income tax business. In addition, I was still deeply involved with my mother and Aaron's activities. Lastly, there was so much snow in February I was snowbound for an entire week.

On March 9, 2008, the front page headline of *The Columbus Dispatch* read, "Blizzard of 2008, Everyone's stuck somewhere as record storm taxes folks' patience." This brutally cold, snowy, windy day was also the last day of the trial. The next two days of closing arguments concluded the trial after more than five weeks. The case against Becky, her fate, was now in the hands of the jury.

What a winter this was turning out to be! I was quite concerned about my mother being in that old house all alone. One day, one of her neighbors called to say, "You're mother is outside shoveling the snow and ice off her driveway!" No matter how often I pleaded with my mother not to go out in the snow and ice, she did it anyway. So far, she had been very lucky and had not ended up in the hospital or worse.

On Thursday, March 13th, the morning *Dispatch* reported that the jury was "still out." Along with another horrible picture of Becky, the headline on the front page of the Business section reported, "Defendants' lives weren't always cushy, lawyers say."

The article also reported, "Parrett was born on the other side of the river in West Virginia to parents 'who barely had an eighth-grade education,' her attorney, Greg Peterson, said. The family moved to Columbus, and she graduated from Franklin Heights High School."

My mother was terribly hurt by those words about her lack of education. My father was deceased, but my mother was still very much alive and being torn apart emotionally.

After a day and a half of deliberation, the jury of eight women and four men came back with a determination of "Guilty" on all counts. The verdict was unanimous. Later that afternoon, Becky phoned; I could tell she had been crying. She said, "I am shocked at the verdict. I'd like to have dinner with you and Mom. Can you pick up Mom and meet me at the Clarmont Restaurant around six?"

I said, "Absolutely. We'll be there. I'm really sorry, Becky. Have you told mom, yet?"

"I wanted to phone you first. Do you think you could go over there? I'm not sure how she's going to react. She's been through so much," she replied.

"Yes," I said. "I'll go right over, but you need to phone her before she hears it on television. That would not be good."

"I know," she said. "I'm calling her as soon as we hang up."

After hanging up the phone, I steadied myself on a nearby table. My legs grew weak; I was so stunned. As tears began rushing down my face, I sat down at the table, put my head in my hands, and cried at length. I was in denial that it was actually happening. My sister, Becky was going to prison!

Many times since the collapse of NCFE more than five years ago, I tried to decide whether Becky was innocent or guilty. I remembered a conversation with her on the way to the airport one day.

"The government offered me a four-year prison sentence if I would plead guilty. I told them I was not going to spend *one* day in jail for something I didn't do. I am innocent and I'm going to prove it!" She said she fired her attorney at that time because he wanted her to accept the plea bargain.

I was so afraid the "guilty" verdict was going to be the last straw for my mother. I needed to get over to her house right away; she would be in agony. I had to pull myself together for my mother's sake. No one in our family had ever been in jail. Soon, Becky would be going to prison. It just did not seem real!

When I arrived, my mother was lying on her bed, sobbing loudly. My heart ached for her. Her oldest child, Dan was gone, and now Becky was going to be taken away, too.

"Come on, Mom. You have to stay strong. You have three little babies who depend on you, have you fed the kitties?" I offered. "We need to get ready, so we can meet Becky for dinner. She's counting on us."

With that, she got up and began to calm down a little bit. I knew that making her feel needed would snap her out of her deep despair. My mother had been a caretaker all her life. If she was needed, she was there.

Becky was already at the Clarmont restaurant when we arrived. She was smiling and seemed extremely calm under the circumstances. After hugs and kisses, we were seated for dinner. Becky looked understandably tired. She talked about the trial and her disappointment that the jury found everyone "guilty across the board" so quickly. She felt the jury did not understand the complexity of the issues. She said she actually saw some of their eyes closed, occasionally, when she looked their way.

"The jurors," she told us, "considered all the defendants 'guilty by association' to Lance Poulsen, the company CEO, who prosecutors said orchestrated the scheme." She said she wished, now, that she had insisted on a separate trial instead of being lumped in with all the others.

Becky was prepared to go to prison. I'll never forget her final words to my mother and me that evening. She said, "I'm really glad this thing is finally over! It's been over five years now. I have my faith, and I'm going to write a book. I'm ready to go; I'm really looking forward to some peace."

The next morning Becky and her attorney, Greg Peterson, were to appear before Judge Algenon L. Marbley. Becky told us that she would, most likely, go directly to jail. She said she would give us a call, if she could, after she met with the judge. We said our goodbyes as we cried together.

Flight Risk
March 14, 2008

T *he Columbus Dispatch's* front page headline reported on March 14, 2008: "Guilty, guilty, guilty, guilty...5 National Century executives face prison time for fraud." The article stated, "It seemed the jury had little doubt about the guilt of the former National Century executives accused of the nation's biggest private fraud. The verdict read: Rebecca (Becky) S. Parrett, 59, of Carefree, Arizona, 9 counts - 20 to 75 years. Sentencing is expected in about three months."

According to the newspaper, after the verdicts, Prosecuting Attorney Doug Squires asked that the executives, who were free on bond during the trial, be imprisoned immediately, saying "they all are flight risks."

It was early afternoon on Friday when Becky called me. She, along with the other four executives, had appeared before Judge Marbley that morning. According to Becky, since she and her former husband, Don Ayers were now retired, Becky retired in 2001, they were put on *house arrest*. The other three executives were allowed to continue working until sentencing. All five were to be equipped with electronic monitoring devices. The judge gave Becky permission to travel to her home in Arizona to receive her monitoring device. She was to remain under house arrest in Arizona until sentencing, several months in the future. She told me she was thrilled she would be able to spend those few months at home with her husband, Gary, and her four dogs and five cats. She asked if I would be willing to take her to the airport for her last flight home.

"I just can't believe they didn't send us directly to jail…and that I get to go home!"

I, too, thought it was unusual that she was allowed so much freedom after being convicted of a federal crime. It never happened that way in the movies.

At the airport, I dropped her at the departure gate and said, "See you in a few months. Call and let us know you got home all right." That was the last time I ever saw my sister, Becky.

R&R
March 16, 2008

Sunday around noon, I was driving to my mother's house when my cell phone rang. It was Becky, and she sounded depressed. She said her plane to Arizona had been delayed; she had not gotten home until the wee hours of the morning on Saturday. She told me she was calling from her car, on her way to Sedona, Arizona because she needed to get some peace for a few days. She said she needed to try to get her head on straight.

"Everything seems so unreal," Becky expressed, "like I'm in the middle of a nightmare, and I can't wake up!"

Sedona is noted for its soothing atmosphere and beautiful landscapes; it is considered to be a spiritual place by many. Several years ago, I passed through Sedona and found all the descriptions to be true. Becky had been to Sedona on prior occasions for rest and relaxation. It is a magnificent place, and it made sense to me she would want to go there.

"Don't worry," Becky said over the phone. "I just need to get away for a few days." She said she was going to call my mother as soon as she got off the phone with me. Then, she was going to turn her phone off. That was the last time I spoke with Becky for a very long time.

When I arrived at my mother's house, she was still in her pajamas and robe. I said, "Why aren't you dressed? Didn't you go to church today?"

"No. I didn't want all those people staring at me and asking questions. I'm so embarrassed. Besides, I can't sleep for thinking about Becky. I'm so worried about her, and I'm so tired." She started crying again and said, "I guess the government will take my house now! I don't want to move! Will I have to move right away?"

"Mom, let's talk about that after you get some rest. Why don't you lie down for a while?"

"Will you stay 'till I get back up?"

"Sure, Mom, I'll be right here."

My Sister is Missing
March 18, 2008

Two days later, the thought occurred to me, "It's Tuesday; wasn't Becky supposed to report to the Arizona authorities to be put on house arrest Monday, yesterday?" I tried calling her cell phone, but there was no answer. After a few more tries with no response, I phoned Gary. No answer there. Then I phoned Bobby, her son. No answer there either. On Wednesday afternoon, I was beginning to get concerned when I hadn't heard back from anyone.

Finally, Gary phoned. He said, "I just now got your message. I'm in the hospital here in Phoenix, all banged up from an accident on my motorcycle. My head is banged up pretty good; my arm is broken, and my Harley is totaled. My family is here with me, and my daughter just brought my cell phone to me today. So, I just now got your messages."

"How and when did it happen?" I asked him.

"They told me it happened on Sunday, but I haven't been able to remember anything that happened since the accident." He replied.

I expressed my concerns about Becky. He said, "I'm sure she's fine. She wasn't supposed to report until today, and she has plenty of time; it's still early here."

"Oh, okay," I said. "Mom is really worried about her. So, tell Becky to phone as soon as she can. And you get better, you hear?"

We hung up, and I said aloud, "Something is not right here."

My intuition was right! In the days that followed, I tried calling Becky many times but never got an answer. I spoke with Gary and Bobby a number of times too, but no one had heard from Becky.

My mother had not heard from Becky, either. She thought Becky was dead! She became more and more nervous and depressed. Her health was in serious decline; some tests ordered by her neurologist confirmed that she had suffered at least two mini strokes in the recent past. Additionally, her Alzheimer's was getting worse by the day. She began to repeat herself over and over. While I was concerned for Becky, I did not think she was dead; I was concerned about my mother's life, however. I feared there was a strong possibility she was going to have a heart attack or stroke due to the stress and worry she was facing. I was truly scared I was going to lose her.

Meanwhile, my head was also spinning with suspicions of what could have happened to Becky. I suddenly remembered something she had divulged on one of those many trips to or from the airport during the time leading up to her trial. Becky had said, "I just heard that one of National Century's Outside Directors, Hal Pote, died in a swimming accident off the coast of Turkey, but the body has not been found. Hal was with Chase Bank, and the bank owns twenty percent of NCFE. He was a board member and Chairman of the NCFE Audit Committee." She paused for a moment; then she said, "I don't believe for one minute that he's dead. He just decided to disappear in order to escape criminal charges."

Recalling that disclosure, I began to wonder if that was exactly what Becky had decided to do, escape?

Runaway Train Gathers Steam
March 27, 2008

T wo weeks after Becky failed to show up to be fitted for the electronic monitor, a warrant was issued for her arrest. The front page headline of *The Columbus Dispatch* Business section, March 29, 2008 read, "Warrant Out for Missing National Century Exec."

Greg Peterson, Becky's attorney, said he was "concerned about her well-being." The article also stated Becky had posted a $100,000 bond and had surrendered her passport to court officials.

Later that same day, Attorney Peterson phoned to tell me about the warrant. He also asked if I'd heard anything at all from Becky. Two others phoned me that day with the same question, Keith Manfra, from the U.S. Pre-Trial Service and Drew Shadwick, U.S. Marshal. All of them wanted to know if I had been contacted by Becky, or if she had contacted our mother. I told them about my last phone conversation with Becky on Sunday, March 16th, and about the later conversation with Gary.

In the days that followed, the newspapers and television news shows were full of Becky's picture, articles about her arrest, and her subsequent disappearance. Oh, how I wished there was some way to keep the constant barrage of bad news away from my mother! She was exceptionally fragile right now and afraid her baby daughter was dead! The atmosphere surrounding our close family and friends was filled with deep sorrow and tears, as if we were mourning the death of a child. Thankfully, Aaron was very busy with school events surrounding his final days before graduation, just weeks away. I could see no benefit in discussing the awful news about Becky with him; he hardly knew her.

Last fall, I took Aaron, my mother and Sonny Boy on a road trip to southern Ohio for a photo shoot of Aaron. Nowadays, most high school seniors want professional photos, name cards, and other items for their high school year book, and graduation announcements for distribution to family and friends. It was a long distance to travel, over 100 miles, but it was worth it. It was a big deal to Aaron and a fun, getaway day for all of us. My uncle, Jack Mayes owns Main Street Photography Studio in Point Pleasant, WV, my home town, located across the Ohio River from Gallipolis, Ohio. I actually grew up in Henderson, WV, which is just across another river, the Kanawha, from Point Pleasant. According to local history, Indians called the site where two rivers meet, "a pleasant point" thus the name Point Pleasant. Somehow, Aaron and I managed to get everything done for his upcoming graduation.

A few days later, on April 2nd, Judge Marbley ordered the arrests of the other four National Century executives who were free pending sentencing. *The Columbus Dispatch* reported, "The executives had a plan to flee to the Caribbean Island of Aruba if convicted. A court hearing is likely to officially revoke their bonds."

I had been checking the pre-paid, disposable phone, the one Becky had asked me to purchase a long time ago. There were no recorded messages or texts. Then, one day, there it was, a text message from Becky! All it said was, "I'm OK. Tell no one."

I couldn't believe my eyes! Overwhelmed with joy and confusion, I didn't know what to do. Becky was alive; at least that was good news. But, what should I do? I knew I had to tell my mother. I immediately got into the car and drove to her house. When she opened the door to let me in, I smiled a huge smile. Then, I looked her straight in the eyes and said, "Mom, Becky is alive! I just now heard from her, and I rushed right over here to tell you. But you can't tell anyone! Do you understand?"

My mother began to cry, happy tears, tears of relief. She did not understand what a "text message" was, so I showed her the message on the phone. She asked me a torrent of questions about Becky until I stopped her and said, "Mom, this is all there is." I continued, "Becky sent this message to me on this special phone. She's the only one who has the phone number for this phone, so it can only be from her. She is obviously alive and well. I'm sure she'll contact us again. In the meantime, you must not tell anyone about this, okay?"

"I don't understand, but I won't tell anyone," she said. I gave her a big hug and gently suggested, "Now, go lie down and get some rest."

The very next day, Aunt Clara called. "Nellie said you'd heard from Becky. Is that right?"

Frustrated that I had to lie, I said, "Clara, I've been so worried about my mother that I just made up a story to make her feel better." I didn't know what else to say. My mother didn't mention it again which was most likely due to her short-term memory loss, the progression of Alzheimer's.

A few days later, my mother phoned and was very upset. On top of everything else, she had just received a late payment notice regarding the PT Cruiser Becky had leased in my mother's name. Very old-fashioned about a lot of things, one of which was the importance of paying your bills on time, she wailed, "What am I going to do? I don't even want this car!" She had forgotten she signed the paperwork when Becky leased the car.

"Calm down, Mom. I'll take care of it," I said, as I gently eased her down into a nearby chair.

After some research, I discovered Becky had leased the PT in 2006, in my mother's name. I did not understand why she had not put it in her own name. The lease contract stated there were two years and a few months remaining on the lease. In order to get out from under the lease, it was going to cost several thousand dollars. Since my mother was not in a financial position to honor the lease, the only possible solution I could see was for me to buy the car. My vehicle at the time was a 1994 red Honda Del Sol convertible which I loved. There was no point in owning two cars, however. So, after fourteen years, my beloved Honda would have to go.

Newspapers and local television stations continued to publish frequent articles regarding National Century executives. On April 28th, a portion of *The Columbus Dispatch* front page article stated, "NATIONAL CENTURY: Prosecutors look to take executives' homes, cars...prosecutors will be going for 'every last penny' the defendants have. ...it is obvious that prosecutors have their sights on the defendants' homes, no matter whose name is on the deed.

If the judge agrees, the government could take her property even though Parrett disappeared in March and remains at large,' Parrett's attorney, Greg Peterson said. 'He can proceed with her in absentia.' "

When my mother saw this article in the paper she became very frightened. She was afraid the government would "set her and her cats out on the street without any notice whatsoever."

"The government doesn't care about me!" She cried, "They can do anything they want. It's all about the money." Reluctantly, she agreed to move in with me.

A few days later, she phoned, crying. She had decided she was not going to move out of her house. I didn't know what I was going to do with her! She was worrying me to death. Her neurologist recently told her she should "no longer be living by herself." It was just a matter of time until she would have to move in with me. I could only hope and pray nothing bad would befall her in the meantime.

She was so confused, nervous and depressed. I wasn't sure that I would be able to handle her when the time did come for her to move in with me. Mercifully, Sheri offered to fly to Columbus from California just to help move my mother into the big house in Grove City. She knew it was not going to be a picnic getting my mother to move anywhere, anytime. Since Sheri's position as payroll administrator only allowed her to take time off during certain days of the month, she and I decided to set the moving date for the first week in October, ready or not. That would give me five months to get my mother packed up.

America's Most Wanted
May 3, 2008

Wen I thought matters could not get much worse, Becky was featured on the television show, *America's Most Wanted,* in May, and again in June. The May segment was titled, "Multi-Billion Dollar Fraudster on the Run." A summary of the segment read, "U.S. Marshals are searching for a grandmother who is facing 75 years in prison and $2.5 million in fines: Rebecca Parrett was convicted by a jury of her peers for her role in the $3 billion collapse of the company she helped found. Now, cops say she took advantage of the system and slipped away before an ankle bracelet could be attached to her."

As far as I know, my mother did not see the shows. She did, however, read an article in *The Columbus Dispatch,* May 3, 2008, entitled, "Fugitive Exec on *America's Most Wanted*". The article featured a picture of Becky, listed the names of Becky's six previous husbands, and stated she had a parrot tattoo on her left arm. The tattoo was a complete surprise to me. The article also stated, "The U.S. Marshals Service has a reward for information that leads to her arrest, although officials won't say how much it is worth."

On Sunday, May 18th, *The Columbus Dispatch* published another news story about Becky entitled, "Where is showy fugitive? Her past yields few clues."

This article contained information reported by her son, Bobby (Rob). It was new information to me.

On May 31st, Aaron graduated from Grove City High School. He was ecstatic and I was so very proud of him. Shortly after graduation, he decided to return to Georgia to attend college. Everything happens for a reason. Soon, my mother was going to need a great deal more of my time.

I continued to check the pre-paid phone, almost daily, hoping for another message from Becky. It had been at least eight weeks since the first text message. Then, once again, there it was, a voice message this time. The message said, "I've been trying to reach you and have just about given up hope. I'll try calling every Sunday around noon until, hopefully, I will reach you. Sure do hope you get this message. I'm fine. Be sure to delete."

There was no doubt in my mind that it was Becky's voice. I rushed over to my mother's house immediately and played the voice message for her over and over again. She was so happy! I told my mother, "I'll be here, this coming Sunday before noon, so you can talk to Becky." Then I added, "Now Mom, you can't tell anyone about this phone call. Do you understand? If you do, Becky will get in serious trouble."

My mother was all smiles. She shook her head and said, "Yes. I understand; I won't tell anyone. I promise."

When Becky phoned on Sunday, my mother and I both talked with her, but only for a few minutes. I think Becky was afraid to be on the phone for very long. I don't know what she said to our mother, but she was smiling from ear to ear during the call.

To me, Becky said, "I was just about to give up trying to reach you. It's so good to hear your voice. I'll try to call you about once a month, on Sundays around noon your time. So, make sure you have your phone turned on. I won't be able to talk long. Gotta go now. Talk to you soon."

Box of Surprises
July 2008

In late July, Gary phoned to arrange a time to drop off boxes Becky wanted me to have. He was also bringing two of Becky's cats. He decided he could no longer care for her animals and was going to find homes for all of them. I told him I would take the two oldest cats, Sammy and Chiquita. They had been members of the family for approximately seventeen years; I could not bear the thought of them going to an unfamiliar, new home.

Most of the boxes contained items I had no use for: cosmetics, dancing shoes, towels, etc. I took an entire carload to the local abused women's shelter where everything was really appreciated, especially the twenty-nine pairs of shoes. Several weeks later, I came upon a large envelope with my name on it in one of the boxes. Inside, there was a disc and letters from Becky addressed to her son, Bobby, our mother, Becky's best friend, Gwen* and me.

The letter to me was dated Saturday, March 15, 2008, just two days after Becky's conviction. It began, "If my disc makes its way back to you, I hope and pray you will help me. You're the only one who can do this for me."

The disc contained a manuscript entitled, *Victim of Justice.* In the letter she wrote to me, Becky asked me to deliver letters to my mother and Gwen as soon as I found them but to hold on to Bobby's for a while. He had a history of alcoholism and just "couldn't be trusted, right now," she wrote. The rest of the letter was full of requests, things Becky wanted me to do for her regarding her manuscript.

The names of some individuals have been changed. Such names are indicated by an asterisk the first time each appears in the narrative.

The next time Becky phoned, she asked me to write down an email address along with a password. She said we could communicate without actually sending the emails. When she wanted to get a message to me, she would save her message as a draft email without sending it. Then, I would access the same email account, read the draft message she had written and delete it. That way, the email was never actually sent through the internet system and remained private. "Wow," I thought, "What a clever idea."

She informed me, "This is a safer way to communicate than by telephone. And don't use your home computer. Go to a public library or someplace like Kinko's." After that day, we seldom spoke by phone. Occasionally, Becky would call just to talk to my mother.

Long before her conviction, Becky had been working on *Victim of Justice*. "The manuscript," she affirmed, "will prove my innocence." Since her disappearance, she had made a lot of changes to the manuscript; she sent her latest version to me via email. For the next few months, our email communications were all about perfecting the manuscript, getting it printed and into the hands of some very influential people. Except for a few items, it was ready to print. Her plan and only hope for freedom, she wrote, was for me to get copies of the manuscript printed and delivered to her best friend, Gwen. One copy was for

Gwen and the other was for Gwen to give to her good friend, Bob Bennett.

Bennett had been a close friend of Gwen's for many years. I met him a few times when he accompanied Gwen to some of our special family celebrations. In one of her emails to me, Becky pointed out that Bennett was the "Chairman of the Ohio Republican Party and a close friend of George W. Bush, the President." Becky also wrote in the email, "I am optimistic Gwen's relationship with Bob might open a door to get help. He's a powerful man in Washington and maybe he can somehow help me." Timing was crucial, she advised; elections were coming up in November. Becky's hope was, if Bob could get a copy of Becky's manuscript into the hands of President Bush prior to the President's exit from office, there was a possibility she could receive a pardon. Typically, a slate of criminals was given pardons prior to a U.S. President leaving office.

I thought, "How great it would be, for Mom's sake, if Becky was pardoned." According to Becky, I was her only hope. If this was the only way, then I would do everything in my power to help. So, on top of everything else going on in my life, I began to work hard in order to complete the manuscript quickly. As Becky had instructed, I read it first, made a few corrections in grammar and spelling, and began contacting others for their input.

Among her many requests, Becky asked me to contact Reverend Darryl Delhousaye, President of the Phoenix Seminary. Prior to her conviction, Becky told him she was working on a book, and he had offered to write something inspirational for it. I contacted Reverend Delhousaye and told him what I was attempting to do. We had a very nice, long conversation. He asked me to send him a copy of the manuscript, which I did. He said he would read it and call me back.

A few weeks later, he phoned, and we talked for quite a while. He seemed like a very nice person. He said, "I feel like I know you, somewhat, from our conversations, and I hope you don't mind what I'm about to say." He continued, "At your age, you have your hands full right now, and your top priority is your mother. It says in the *Bible* to 'Honor your father and your mother', but nowhere in the *Bible* does it say that you are supposed to honor your sister."

"Becky's book has twice as many pages as it should have," he stated. "She keeps repeating herself. To quote an old saying, 'Me thinks she doth protest too much.' Many innocent people end up in prison; they write books and file appeals. Becky is a fugitive. As President of the Seminary, I'm sorry, but I am not in a position to help her," Delhousaye said, then added, "Wherever she is, I pray she is well. Good luck, Linda. And take good care of your mother."

When I hung up the phone, I began to cry. The reverend's words about "not honoring your sister" kept going over and over in my mind. What was I doing? Was I doing the right thing, here? Where I come from, we were taught to protect our family, no matter what. That is the way I was raised – family comes first. Becky insisted I was the only one who could help her. What about the promise I made to my brother, Dan? I decided I simply had to honor Becky's request to get a copy of her manuscript into the hands of Bennett and, hopefully, President Bush. They were the most important people on the list.

She also requested that I print a few copies for family members. So, a few days later, I had ten copies printed and bound at a local office supply store. Each copy contained 262 pages. I gave Gwen the letter Becky wrote to her, along with two copies of the manuscript, one for her and one for Bennett. The copies to family members, I would disseminate later.

A Slippery Slope
August - September 2008

Another of Becky's requests was that I contact an attorney named Dick Riley* in the Cincinnati area. In a recent phone conversation with Becky, she gave me Dick's phone numbers and asked me to give him a call.

"You can trust Dick," Becky avowed, "We went to high school together and have remained friends over the years." She continued, "I'd like for you to share the manuscript with him and see if he can reserve a website domain name for *Victim of Justice*. In the event something good happens with the manuscript, it would be nice to help others who have been victims as well."

Sometime during the last week in August, I phoned Dick Riley's office in Cincinnati. When Dick answered the phone, I said, "Hi. This is Becky's sister, Linda. I wonder if I could meet with you sometime to discuss some matters regarding our mother." It was obvious by the sound of his voice he was surprised to hear from me. He agreed to meet with me and suggested meeting at a Cracker Barrel Restaurant approximately half-way between Columbus and Cincinnati. He said that restaurant was where he and Becky met many times over the years prior to Becky's disappearance. We set the date for September 3, 2008 at 6:30 p.m.

Dick recognized me immediately; he said we had met once before, years earlier. I could tell he was delighted to see me. He was very handsome. Becky had shared with me that, during the 1970s, she and Dick had engaged in a sexual relationship and had continued to have an "on-again, off-again affair since high school." She also mentioned he had acted as her attorney on various small legal matters unrelated to the NCFE case.

Before I disclosed the real reason for our meeting, I told him I wanted our meeting to be confidential, and I wanted him to send me a bill for his services. It was essential to me to ensure we had an attorney/client relationship.

We talked for several hours, mostly about Becky. I told him everything! I gave him a copy of the manuscript, and I explained to him exactly how Becky and I were communicating by phone and with email drafts. I revealed to Dick Riley, "I'm very concerned I will get into trouble for doing something illegal." I felt so relieved when he replied, "Linda, it is not against the law to communicate with a fugitive."

I asked him a couple of questions about the deed transfer and life estate on Elliott Avenue, my mother's house. He said he would do some research and get back to me concerning those topics. I asked him, again, to be sure to send me a bill for his services, so I would have something in writing to protect our attorney/client, confidential relationship. In turn, he asked me to write him a letter and predate it to one week earlier. He said this would confirm, for his records, I had requested his confidential services as an attorney.

Understandably, he wanted to read the manuscript before making any comments on it. Before we parted, he asked for the user name and password of our special email account, so he could contact Becky, too. Then, he wrote something on a small piece of paper, handed it to me and said, "Tell Becky I still remember." There was one word on the paper, "Tigress!"

In the weeks that followed, the three of us, Dick, Becky and myself, communicated using draft messages in the dedicated email account. We denoted who the message was for in the subject line of the email, putting an "R" if the message was for Dick Riley, an "L" for me or a "B" for Becky. After a few weeks, Becky told me she and Dick had set up their own private email account using drafts.

A letter from Dick dated September 26, 2008, revealed information obtained by a title examiner regarding my mother's house. He discovered that a second NOTICE OF LIS PENDENS had been filed by Assistant United States Attorney, Douglas Squires on May 5, 2008. Fortunately, this time the lien had not been hand-delivered to my mother in person.

On September 30, a Legal Notice was posted in the newspaper stating, "Notice of Seizure and Forfeiture of Property Seized: the property is located at 2813 Elliott Avenue, Franklin County, Columbus, Ohio 43204."

I did not show these notices to my mother. I simply told her the government was definitely going to seize the property and it was time for her to move in with me.

She sobbed, "This is my home! I can't believe Becky would let this happen to me. I don't want to leave my home, but I know I have to now." My heart ached for her.

The entire month of September was a rough one in regards to dealing with my mother. One day she called to say her alarm system was going off, and she didn't know what to do. I called the local police, who went right over and shut it off. Another time, she called saying her land-line phone was out of order. After more than an hour on the phone with the phone company service department, it turned out that one of her phones was merely off the hook.

Hurricane Ike came through Columbus that month, too, and my mother lost her electricity for an entire week. Much to my dismay, she insisted on staying in her house with no electricity. She angrily told me she would "never speak to me again if I moved her and her cats in with me." She was really fighting to keep her independence as long as she possibly could. So, I drove to her house every day the electricity was out. I took food, candles and batteries, cleaned out her freezer, etc. It was loads of extra work for me, and it would have been so much easier if she had just moved in with me for a week. She was really giving me grief.

At her neurology appointment that September, the doctor asked her some routine questions. My mother did not know the answer to what year, month or day of the week it was. According to the doctor, these were all symptoms of the dreaded Alzheimer's disease. Although my mother was taking medications to slow the progression of the disease, unfortunately, there was no cure.

As Good As It Gets
October - December 2008

My daughter, Sheri arrived in town on October 8. The very next day, she took my mother and her cats to the big house in Grove City. The moving company and I followed with the rest. It was a very traumatic day for my mother. It would have been impossible without Sheri's help. She and my mother shared a special relationship.

I was relieved to finally have my mother living with me. The entire top level of the big house was now her private domain. We called it "the penthouse". My mother had a living room, bedroom, kitchenette with refrigerator and microwave, a full bathroom and large loft area all for herself and her kitties. It was almost as much space as her entire house on Elliott Avenue. It was a welcome reprieve from shuttling between houses for me. Whenever Becky called, my mother was thrilled to talk to her. I also printed out Becky's emails for my mother to read.

The remainder of the year was so much better than the previous ten months had been. Becky's name and likeness were no longer featured constantly in *The Columbus Dispatch,* and my mother and her cats were beginning to get settled in their new home. We had a nice, quiet Thanksgiving holiday. I cooked a big turkey dinner for all of us, including Aunt Clara, Aunt Pat and a young friend of the family who went to school with my kids. Todd played the guitar, sang for us, and brightened the day for the older ladies with his charming and witty personality.

During the month of December, I planned a small party with my mother as the guest of honor. I drove her to church each week, took her to movies, doctor appointments, and to see the New York City Rockettes perform in Columbus. I also accompanied her to church on Christmas Eve, the Grove City Christmas parade, and the Retired Teamsters Christmas dinner in Plain City. As 2008 drew to a close, my mother and I shared a quiet New Years' Eve champagne toast. It was "as good as it gets" under the circumstances, and I was grateful.

Lost and Broken
2009

O n January 9th, the following appeared in *The Columbus Dispatch,* "Web site of America's Most Wanted' Ex-Dublin Exec a Famous Fugitive. A former Dublin executive who has been on the run for about 10 months, since her conviction in connection with the nation's largest fraud at a privately held company, is featured on the *America's Most Wanted* website. U.S. marshals announced that Rebecca S. Parrett, 60, is the featured fugitive at www.amw.com."

Since my mother was now living with me, I would retrieve the newspaper from the front porch every morning before she came downstairs for breakfast. If Becky's name or picture appeared that day, I would pretend to be reading that section. With her Alzheimer's continually getting worse, she soon forgot about reading the rest of the newspaper. She was still, however, a faithful fan of the morning, midday, and evening television news programs.

The entire month of January 2009 was a flurry with lots of snow and brutally cold temperatures. High temperatures ranged in the teens or single digits and, with wind chill, fell as far as minus 11° on the 16th.

On Sunday, January 25, my mother came down the stairs, fully dressed, and very confidently announced she was going to drive herself to church. She had not driven at all since she moved in with me, almost four months ago. I offered to drive her, as I had done every other Sunday, but she firmly stated, "No.

I'm perfectly capable of driving myself." The sun was out that day, but the temperature was in the teens.

As soon as she left, I phoned Aunt Clara and told her what my mother was attempting to do. We were both concerned she would never make it to the church without getting lost. Since Clara attended the same church, I asked her, "Please, call me if Mom doesn't show up at church by the end of the service." In the meantime, snow began to fall with a vengeance, accumulating rapidly. After the church service ended, Clara phoned with the news my mother had not made it to church. We both feared the worst.

The snow continued to fall, and the temperature outside was dropping. Television and radio weather stations were recommending that citizens "stay off the roads except for an absolute emergency." Since my mother's old house was close to the church, Clara offered to drive there first to see if Mother might possibly have remembered her way there. No such luck; she was not there, either. Aunt Clara, along with Aunt Pat and Troy, Clara's son, began searching for my mother in the now blizzard–like conditions. We decided it would be best if I remained at home in Grove City in case my mother tried to contact me, or by some miracle, found her way back home.

Several years ago, I purchased a cell phone for my mother, specifically to keep with her in case of an emergency, especially when she went out in the car. She repeatedly told me she didn't need or want the phone and only used it to make long distance calls to her sister, Goldie in Florida. She could be so stubborn sometimes! I quickly ran upstairs, hoping to find the cell phone missing from its usual spot on my mother's night stand, but there it was.

Over two hours had now passed with no sign of my mother. I decided it was time to contact the local police departments, and they began to search for my mother, as well. More than four hours had passed when the phone rang. It was Clara. "Nellie is all right," she said. "She's shaken and scared but not injured."

My mother had been lost and finally pulled into a restaurant parking lot, went inside and asked an employee to call Clara. Since the roads were still extremely dangerous, Clara offered to pick her up and bring her home to Grove City. When my mother arrived home, she was very tired, sad and confused. I gave her a big hug and said, "It's okay; I'm so glad you're all right." I did not say anything more to her, but I thought to myself that it was time for her to stop driving before she had an accident and hurt herself or someone else.

The next day, a friend drove me to pick up my mother's car. There was only one small scratch on the side of the car. According to the odometer reading, my mother had driven over sixty miles that Sunday morning – lost and during a blizzard! Normally on Mondays, I worked most of the day at a client's office on the west side. My mother was on my mind a great deal that day. After only a couple of hours, I decided to go straight home. My intuition was right; when I arrived home, I found my mother lying on her back on the kitchen floor. Her eyes were open, and she said, "I tripped over the dog and I can't get up. I've been here for several hours. It hurts when I try to get up."

"Oh, my God, Mom!" I declared, "I have to call 911." Then, I asked her, "Where does it hurt?"

She pointed to her left hip but said, "Don't call 911. Just help me up; I'll be all right."

I started to gently assist her to stand, but she cried out, "Stop. It hurts too much."

I immediately called 911, and the emergency squad was at the door in just a few minutes. It was quickly discovered my mother had broken her hip. I thought it was an exceedingly ironic turn of events. She drove around, lost and in a blizzard, for four hours without hurting herself and, the very next day she trips over the dog at home and breaks her hip. She was admitted to Doctors' Hospital, where she had hip replacement surgery the following day. Three days later, she was transferred to Monterey Rehabilitation Center in Grove City for five weeks of physical therapy and 24-hour care.

In the weeks that followed, Becky and I communicated very infrequently. When we did, it was mostly emails concerning our mother. After the Reverend Delhousaye's statement to me regarding "not honoring your sister," I realized I had done as much as I possibly could for Becky as far as her manuscript was concerned. Hopefully, Mr. Bennett or Attorney Riley would come through for her.

In one of Becky's emails, she asked me to finally give a copy of the manuscript to Bobby along with the letter she had written to him. That was all she wanted him to know. She instructed me not to tell him about our phone or email communication. She said there was no way he could be trusted to know any more than what she had included in the letter and manuscript. So, I mailed these to Bobby along with a note asking him to phone me, so I could talk to him on a phone that was not being tapped. I was fairly certain that my home and cell phones were being tapped simply due to my family relationship to Becky. Up to this point, the only time I had spoken to the marshals was by telephone in the few weeks immediately following Becky's disappearance, almost a year ago. I made no false statements to the marshals in those phone calls since Becky had not yet contacted me. Now, since I knew it was not against the law to communicate with Becky, I simply did not want to volunteer information to the marshals for fear they would prevent me from accomplishing my goal of trying to help Becky receive a Presidential pardon.

About a week later, Bobby called me at work. I explained to him Gary had delivered the boxes to me containing the letters and manuscript, along with the cats. He sounded understandably sad and depressed. I felt sorry for Bobby; he had depended on his mother during his entire, luxurious life, and now he was practically destitute. I tried to reassure him, somewhat, by saying, "Bobby, I'm certain that your mother is alive and well." We talked for just a few minutes, but before hanging up, I said to him, "Now don't forget, Bobby. I'm trying to help get a Presidential pardon for your mother. So please, whatever you do, don't tell anyone about this for a while. Okay?"

The cold winter month of February was almost as brutal as January. Daily temperatures stayed in the teens for the entire month. In addition to working with my income tax and other business clients, and supervising matters regarding my mother's stay at Monterey Rehab Center, I spent countless hours at the local Medicaid office. With a new hip replacement and Alzheimer's, my mother was going to need care twenty-four hours a day, seven days a week once she was released from Monterey. Neither my mother nor I had the financial means to hire someone to be there with her while I worked. We were counting on Medicaid to fill that gap. My mother had no funds to fall back on, not even her house which she had deeded to Becky. The gold coins and cash, thousands of dollars

Dan had given to my mother for her retirement had also been given to Becky by our mother. It was still incomprehensible to me that Becky had not established some sort of financial estate plan for our mother's long-term care, just in case she was convicted and unable to care for her as expected.

After interminable hours of paperwork and appointments at the local Medicaid office, my mother's claim was rejected for Medicaid assistance. The reason, according to Medicaid: in reviewing her bank statements for the previous five years, there were thousands of dollars that had been deposited in a savings account in her name and subsequently withdrawn. Since we could not prove where the money had gone, her claim was denied.

My mother told me it was Becky's money. Becky's name was also on that savings account. When I checked the bank statements to refute the claim, I saw thousands of dollars had been deposited into the account and withdrawn just prior to Becky's trial and conviction. Before my mother would be able to qualify for Medicaid assistance, there would have to be what they called a "spend-down" of that money. I was beginning to get very concerned. How was I going to work and take care of my mother without some outside help?

On March 6, my mother was discharged from Monterey Rehab Center. From that point on she had to use a walker or a cane; her surgery and age also necessitated physical therapy at home for an indefinitely long time. Fortunately, the physical therapy was covered by Medicare. The next few months would have been completely unmanageable for me if it were not for the help offered by my mother's closest friends, Willa, Ivy and Anna. They stayed with my mother several hours each week while I worked and ran errands. I was exceptionally grateful to them.

I continued to be angry at Becky for being so selfish and inconsiderate when it came to our mother's long term care needs. With Dan gone, Becky knew I did not have the financial resources to care for our mother properly on my own. Becky also knew she might be convicted and thereby unable to fulfill the previously understood plan of caring for our mother. In spite of these undeniable truths, and with full awareness that she held all of our mother's assets, Becky still did nothing to safeguard my mother's future care. I tried my best during these times to live by a quote I came across by Virginia Satir, an author and psychotherapist, "Life is not the way it's supposed to be, it's the way it is. The way you cope with it is what makes the difference. "

U.S. Marshals' Visit
March 9 - 27, 2009

Early one picturesque, winter morning, two United States Marshals appeared at my front door. Before inviting Marshals Shadwick and Ralston inside, I stepped outside and asked if they were bringing bad news concerning Becky; I was trying to spare my mother any further upset. I explained to them my mother had been home only three days, after spending the previous five weeks at Monterey Rehab Center recovering from hip surgery. I further communicated she also suffered from Alzheimer's disease, and her condition was extremely fragile at this time. Any bad news regarding her daughter, Becky might be more than she could cope with at this point. When they declared they were, "just conducting follow-up interviews," I invited them inside.

After introducing them to my mother who was sitting at the kitchen table, I promptly suggested I escort my mother to her upstairs room, which I did. When I returned, Marshal Shadwick informed me it was a "felony to provide false information or conceal important facts from a federal law enforcement officer."

"I didn't know that," I said.

Ever since Attorney Riley had assured me it was not against the law to communicate with a fugitive, I was no longer concerned I was breaking any law by maintaining communication with Becky. I was further encouraged of the legality of such communication by the fact Riley now communicated with Becky, as well. However, I was worried if the marshals knew I was in communication with her, they would pressure me to trap or trick her in some way or get her to reveal her whereabouts. I was conflicted, but determined to protect my family, especially my frail mother.

Shadwick asked me to repeat my recollection of the events surrounding Becky's disappearance, which I did. I reported the same facts I had given to him during a phone interview back in March 2008, just a couple weeks after Becky's disappearance.

Then, he asked me if I had heard anything else from Becky since the phone call on the Sunday following her conviction.

I answered, "I have not."

Did I hesitate at that moment? Did I falter the first time I actually lied to the marshals? I do not remember.

Before that one, single untruth, I had answered all of their direct questions truthfully. I did not, however, volunteer any additional information they left unasked. Before that day, I felt secure in the knowledge I was not being unlawful by engaging in ongoing phone and email contact with my sister. I certainly had moments of doubt about my decision to do so, but they were trumped by the obvious benefit the contact had on my mother's health and the hope I was helping my sister obliquely to prove her own innocence. For, no matter the pain she had inflicted on me, Becky was still my sister, my family, my blood.

The rest of the interview went quickly. Shadwick asked if I had stayed in contact with Gary Green and Robert Parrett, Becky's son, Bobbie. I reported, truthfully, that we spoke occasionally by telephone and that Gary had driven the U-Haul truck containing boxes and two of Becky's Siamese cats to Columbus. I did not mention Becky's manuscript, or the very personal letters she had written to family and her friend.

After the Marshals departed, Shadwick's statement, "…providing false information or concealing important facts…" began to bother me. Until Marshal Shadwick made that statement so emphatically, I did not think I was doing anything wrong because Attorney Riley had assured me that communicating with Becky was not against the law. It just did not occur to me until this interview that it was against the law to conceal facts from a federal law enforcement officer.

My head was spinning with questions. "Am I really doing something wrong?" I reflected. Here I was, in my own house, not under any kind of oath. I never knew where Becky was physically located. Was I supposed to turn my sister in? Was I supposed to rat on my sister? I was raised to protect my family. I was trying to help Becky get a Presidential pardon, and I believed I was keeping my mother alive by enabling her to speak to Becky, the daughter she had feared dead.

"After all," I thought, "communicating with Becky was not actually hindering the marshals' search for her. Why should I volunteer to help them instead of helping my sister?" It was inconceivable to me that I could go to prison for protecting my family in this manner.

A couple of weeks later, Marshal Shadwick asked if I would mind coming downtown to his office for another interview on Friday, March 27, at noon. When I arrived, I was taken into a small office where I was seated at a table across from Shadwick. The only thing on the table was a tape recorder. Marshal Shadwick said nothing. He looked directly into my eyes then turned on the tape recorder. I could not believe my ears. The marshals had taped the phone conversation between Bobby and I wherein we discussed his mother's manuscript and letters. Bobby, my own nephew, had set me up! He told the marshals everything I asked him to keep confidential – the existence of the manuscript, the letters to family and Becky's friend.

After listening to the taped conversation, I told Shadwick I had not mentioned Becky's manuscript before because I was worried I would get in trouble for distributing printed material full of anti-government statements and accusations. I explained to him how I had come across the envelope containing the CD and letters in one of the boxes brought to me by Gary.

Marshal Shadwick repeatedly asked me whether Becky had left money behind to take care of our mother. I suspected he did not believe me when I explained my mother's current financial position and how she got in that position.

"Basically," I answered, "Because my mother gave everything she had to Becky, now she has nothing." I agreed it was hard to believe that Becky, who had so much, left nothing behind for her mother. It was still hard for me to accept as true.

Shadwick ended our meeting by saying he would stop by my house on Monday to pick up a copy of everything Becky had left behind related to the manuscript.

When I arrived back at my car in the parking garage, I quickly opened the door and collapsed onto the front seat. Tears were streaming down my face and I was shaking all over; the interview had been brutal, and I had not seen it coming. What an ordeal! What had I gotten myself into?

At this point, I knew I could be in serious trouble for concealing the fact I was communicating with Becky. I was so frustrated and hurt by the difficulties Becky's disappearance had caused my mother and me. It felt enormously unfair she would put her family in jeopardy by initiating and maintaining contact with us, let alone asking me to help her with the manuscript. I still could not believe Bobby set me up. I made up my mind, right then and there, that I was not going to mention that manuscript to another soul. I had tried my best to get a pardon for Becky. From now on, I was done with that manuscript! I was done with Bobby, too!

I was suddenly and painfully reminded of a quote I have lived by throughout my entire life, "To try and fail, is at least to learn; to fail to try is to suffer the inestimable loss of what might have been!" Chester Barnard, author.

Violated and Abused
March 27 - April 30, 2009

Another article, including pictures, appeared on March 27th in *The Columbus Dispatch* with the headline screaming, Fugitive National Century Exec gets 25 Years. The article read, "Rebecca Parrett was sentenced in absentia this morning to 25 years in federal prison for nine fraud-related charges, including money laundering, in the National Century Financial Enterprises scam. Parrett, a company founder, disappeared soon after she was convicted last March." Details of the article included a fierce comment from U.S. District Judge, Algenon L. Marbley:

'I believe, as justice is always served, she will be found,' U.S. District Judge Algenon L. Marbley said before the sentencing. 'White collar offenses cause as much damage to society as those perpetrated by blue-collar or street criminals.' He also ordered her to pay restitution, along with the other defendants, of $2.4 billion. Marbley said that on all levels, Parrett, who is now 60, was one of the people in charge of carrying out the fraud. Marbley ruled earlier that the government could seize nearly $400,000 that Parrett had in an account in Arizona. Her attorney, Gregory Peterson, said he learned about the money only after she disappeared.

On March 28th, the U.S. District Court in Columbus, Ohio issued a warrant for the arrest of Rebecca Parrett for violating the conditions of her post-trial release.

On March 30, Marshals Shadwick and Ralston stopped by the house in Grove City to pick up a copy of the manuscript and letters from Becky. I was unaware at the time but found out later, on that same day, the marshals also went to southern Ohio to interview Attorney Dick Riley. The following information is paraphrased from the marshals' official "Report of Investigation". As soon as the marshals arrived, Attorney Riley said his ability to speak with the officers would be very much limited due to attorney client privilege. Early on in the interview, Attorney Riley said he had no idea where Becky was, or if she was alive. He said he had not had contact with her since her disappearance. Riley said he had not talked to her "in a very long time," and did not know how to contact her. When asked, Attorney Riley confirmed he had engaged in a sexual relationship with Becky during the 1970s.

Riley told the marshals I sent him a copy of the manuscript, but he only read about twenty pages of it. He disclosed that I asked for his help in getting the manuscript published. Once again, Attorney Riley stated an attorney client privilege applied to his communications with me.

Marshal Shadwick asked whether Becky had ever mentioned the thought of absconding. Riley said she had not. Shadwick then asked Riley if any of the work he did for Becky involved any foreign country. Attorney Riley said it did not. Later in the interview, Shadwick confronted Riley with a document addressed to him from Costa Rican lawyer, Armando Moreno.

Attorney Riley admitted he recognized the document as part of some research he did on Becky's behalf. When Shadwick asked Attorney Riley why he did not bring up the Costa Rican research when asked about foreign countries, Riley bizarrely claimed it was because he thought the research he did was related to Nicaragua.

Toward the end of this initial interview, Shadwick again asked Riley if he had any contact with Becky since she absconded. Attorney Riley then divulged that Becky had, in fact, called him at least a month after the trial. Riley said she had called from an unknown number at his office line. Riley said the conversation lasted between two and ten minutes, and the only thing Becky said was, "I'm alive; I'm okay." Attorney Riley stated this was the entire content of the conversation and that at no time did Becky reveal her location. Shadwick then told Riley to expect a subpoena to be delivered shortly, gave Riley his business card and left Riley's office.

Approximately five minutes after the marshals left Riley's office, Riley called Shadwick and requested that the marshals return to his office. When they did, Attorney Riley admitted to additional contact with Becky since her disappearance. He said he felt conflicted between his obligation to be truthful to the government and his responsibilities to attorney client privilege. Riley admitted he had engaged in multiple "message board" posting exchanges with Becky for a period of about one month. He explained the process of signing in and posting messages for Becky and described how she used the same account to post messages for him to read. Riley reported to the marshals he "learned of this method of contacting Becky from Linda Case." In another interview with Marshal Shadwick, Riley reported that Gary Greene and I were both communicating with Becky via disposable cell phones.

When I contacted Dick Riley initially, the sole purpose was to discuss Becky and her manuscript, as Becky had requested. She advised me, "You can trust Dick." The matter involving my mother's real estate was simply an excuse for his records and to establish our professional, confidential relationship.

"What happened to my attorney client privilege?" I asked myself. It was obvious: Attorney Dick Riley violated my attorney client privilege to get himself off the hook with the U.S. Marshals. Not just once, but on several occasions, Attorney Riley deliberately lied to the U.S. Marshals regarding his communications with Becky after her disappearance.

The weeks that followed were spent mostly dealing with my mother. Afraid to leave her alone, I worked less and less outside my home office. Upon arriving home one day after running a short errand, my neighbor came over to tell me she saw my mother fall on the ice and snow near the mailbox. She watched my mother get up and walk back to the house, so she knew my mother was all right, but she wanted me to be aware. Even though I pleaded with my mother not to go outside with ice and snow on the ground, she simply would not listen.

According to the neurologist, as the Alzheimer's disease progressed, my mother and I would experience what he termed a role reversal; I would become the mother and she would become the child. We were both having a hard time accepting that arrangement. It was a chore for me to even convince her to go to her doctor appointments. She was now seeing three different doctors: the family general practitioner, a neurologist and the orthopedic surgeon. She had not driven her car since the incident in January when she got lost in the snowstorm; I had taken her car keys away. Even though the neurologist told her it was too dangerous for her to drive anymore, she never forgave me for limiting her independence in that way. Each day, my mother seemed to get more and more irritable. She was becoming combative and, occasionally, abusive towards me. I felt the weight of all these combined stressors pushing me to a breaking point.

A Dream Renewed
May 6, 2009

S heri called me from Santa Barbara to say the smoke from the first forest fire of 2009 was so bad she had to close the windows and turn on the air purifier. Her apartment was not in an evacuation warning area but her workplace was. Later that day, Sheri sent an email message that read, "I really would like to come back to Ohio when I get enough dollars and help you get your stuff together, help with grandma and just take a freakin' caravan down to Mexico. Maybe you and I could take a re-con trip ahead of time and leave Albert back to take care of Grandma, the cats and dog? It's hard to settle on a place when you haven't been there."

Sheri and Albert had been saving their money for several years. They discussed opening a business in Mexico where the cost of living was less than half what it was in this country, but it was a "someday" plan.

As fate would have it, less than two weeks later, Sheri received a very large sum of money. She was expecting a reward for reporting a fraudulent employer to the Internal Revenue Service, but almost fainted when the check arrived. She was ecstatic! No more waiting! She and Albert could immediately begin fulfilling their dream of relocating to Mexico. Fortunately for my mother and me, they wanted to take us with them.

Sheri began researching Mexico in earnest, reading books, sending them to me to read, checking out websites and making plans. They decided we should be on the road to Mexico no later than March 1, 2010. Albert's hometown of La Tinaja had a huge celebration each year on the 19th of March. He wanted to be there to celebrate with his family for the first time in ten years.

In her research, Sheri got very excited over the town of Puerto Escondido, a world-renowned surfing destination with a multi-cultural population. In another email she wrote, "I really think this might be it...our 'some beach, somewhere'!" Last September, Sheri sent me a musical birthday card that played an excerpt from the song titled, "Some Beach, Somewhere" by Blake Shelton:

> Warm breezes blowin'
> Palm trees a growin',
> I picture myself right there
> On Some beach...Somewhere!

I loved this card and sang those words hundreds of times over the next few months. March 2010 was only nine months away; there was still a great deal to do.

ABC Producer Visits
May 26, 2009

A letter arrived, addressed to both my mother and I, from Martin Silvestro*, a producer with ABC News in New York. The letter stated, "The ABC News program '20/20' is producing a report on the search for your sister and daughter Ms. Rebecca Parrett. I am writing because I am coming to Ohio next week to meet informally with many of the people involved in the case, and I am hoping you will find time to chat with me." He went on to say, "I'd like the opportunity to take you to dinner or coffee and have an off-the-record conversation, with no cameras involved. I'd like to explain how we plan to move forward with our report and answer any questions you might have." He asked that I phone him to set up a time to get together. By the time the letter arrived, he was already in town, so I suggested we meet the next day for lunch at Spagio's Restaurant in Grandview, Ohio. I explained to him that, due to my mother's broken hip and Alzheimer's, I did not feel it would be in her best interest to join us.

Mr. Silvestro arrived at Spagio's Restaurant sharply dressed in a dark suit and tie, carrying a beautiful bouquet of flowers for my mother. He was exceptionally nice, and very easy to talk to. So easy, in fact, that I invited him to the house to meet my mother later in the day.

He told me he found the story about Becky while searching on the internet, and he was looking to produce a sixty minute segment about her. He said he read a lot of the harsh things written about her, and he was hoping we could give him "an unbiased understanding of who she is, where she came from, and what people should know about her."

Later that evening, my mother and I hosted Martin Silvestro at our home for several hours; we thoroughly enjoyed his company. We shared family pictures, and Mr. Silvestro even played the piano for us. He appeared to be excited about producing a "20/20 Special" about the "positive" side of Becky's life. He said he would come back to Columbus at a later date to tape an interview with me, as well as other family members. The program would probably not be aired until September, he said. Silvestro had met with many others during his two-day stay in Columbus including Becky's attorney, Greg Peterson. He also met with Marshal Shadwick and requested to film some of the Marshals' investigation. Someone told him about Becky's manuscript, and he asked me if he could have a copy. I gave him a copy, praying that I was not getting myself in trouble with the marshals again.

Breakdown
June - October 2009

The first of June, my mother had a breakdown. After another argument because she wanted the keys to her car, she refused to take her medicine, knocked the pills and water out of my hands, and then began hitting me on the shoulders and around my face. She was acting like a crazy person. When she finally calmed down, I phoned her neurologist. He said this was not unusual in Alzheimer's patients, and I should immediately call for an ambulance and have her transported to Riverside Hospital for evaluation. She was later re-admitted to Monterey Care Center. My mother required professional, around-the-clock care, and I simply could not provide it any longer without help. I was ready for a breakdown myself.

Over the next three months, I listed the house for sale with a realtor and began selling my furniture. I bought and learned how to drive an RV and began making all the necessary arrangements in order to travel to Mexico with Sheri and Albert. Out in California, Sheri and Albert began selling their furniture and bought a fifth-wheel travel trailer along with a big truck to pull it. They planned to pull their trailer to Columbus by Christmas in order to help me with last minute arrangements for the trip. Our plan was to leave Ohio no later than March 1, 2010, so Albert would be home in time for the La Tinaja annual celebration on March 19th. After visiting with Albert's family, we planned to travel west, across Mexico to the town of Puerto Escondido, our final destination. After that, my plan was to find a suitable apartment for my mother and me, then fly back to Ohio to get her. The cost of living in Mexico is so much cheaper than the States that we would be able to afford a private nurse for my mother. Sheri and Albert would be close by to help with her as well.

Everyone knew our plans. All of our family, all of our friends, our employers, all knew when and where we were going, even Becky. Becky and I were still keeping in touch, occasionally, via email. I gave her the details of our plans to travel to Mexico. I figured if she was willing to risk getting in touch with us, then that was her business. If she got caught doing it, that was also her business. If the marshals followed me to Mexico and captured Becky, I would not be at all surprised. That was their business. My business was being excited about the possibility of a much better life with my mother, Sheri and Albert. It had been a rough life the past seven years since Dannie died. I was ready for a big change.

By the end of September, four months had gone by since Mr. Silvestro had visited our home. We still had not heard a word from him, so I decided to send him a follow-up email, asking for the status of the "20/20" program. His prompt reply was, "For now, "20/20" has decided to delay production on the story and assign me to other projects they want to air first. Frustrating, I know. I will call you as soon as I have more news." That was the last time we heard from Mr. Silvestro. Someone, apparently, did not want that story to be told; someone with enough authority to stop the production of an ABC News program!

The year was almost gone. It was already October, I thought as I gazed out the kitchen bay window. The leaves on the trees were beginning to change from green into brilliant rustic brown, yellow and orange. As I stood there for a few moments, soaking up this breathtaking scene, I remembered and began to recite aloud, a charming quote from a poem written by James Courtney Challis, "October is the glory and magnificence of the year's late afternoon." I felt that same warm magnificence when my thoughts returned to living in Mexico.

Around mid-month, Aunt Clara and I took my mother on our annual sight-seeing trip through Skyline Drive in Hocking Hills; my mother always enjoyed this outing. The fall leaves and shrubs were at their peak of color and simply magnificent. Our first stop was always the Laurelville Fruit Farm market for Golden Delicious apples, homemade apple butter and freshly made apple cider. After several stops at various types of gift shops, mostly featuring wonderful, hand-crafted items, we would end our day with a tasty home-cooked late lunch at the Old Towne Restaurant in Laurelville. Their home-made pies were always the finishing touch to the memorable day. It was obvious my mother enjoyed the day, but not as much as previous years. This year, she seemed very confused and anxious to return to familiar surroundings at the Monterey Care Center. Even though I knew it was best, it broke my heart she could not come home with me.

Happiness Arrives Early
November - December 2009

S heri and Albert surprised me by showing up the day before Thanksgiving instead of waiting until Christmas. I was so happy to see them. It was really true! We were actually going to Mexico!

It was so wonderful to have some of my immediate family close by again, especially for the Thanksgiving and Christmas holidays. In years past, my house had always been the place where the entire family gathered together to laugh, sing karaoke, play games, exchange gifts, eat, and just talk and enjoy each other's company. We always had a great time. Our family holidays were never the same following the events of 2002, however.

While we were together this year, we reminisced about great Christmases past. The best Christmas ever, at least in my Christmas memory bank, was when my son, Michael rented a large house for a week at Big Bear Resort in California. All three of my children were living in California at that time. Trisha was attending the University of California at Irvine. Mike and Sheri were both single and each had an apartment on the beach in Redondo Beach. When I arrived in Irvine, the temperature was in the seventies. Our first night spent at Big Bear was quite different. The temperature was minus ten degrees with lots of snow. The entire immediate family including Starsky, Sheri's cat, and my one-year-old grandson, Aaron, spent an entire week relaxing by the fireplace, cooking and just being together. Occasionally, we would venture out in the snow to go sledding on a huge rubber raft. What fun we had! Those were, as they say, "the good ole days!"

On the last day of 2009, a spectacular blue moon filled the skies. Sheri, Albert and I attended a New Year's Eve celebration at Crown Plaza starring Mike Albert, a local Elvis impersonator. At the stroke of midnight, I lifted my glass filled with champagne and said to Sheri and Albert, "Here's to the New Year 2010, the best year of our lives!"

I had no idea how untrue that statement would prove to be.

Prep Time
January 2010

There was still so much to do before leaving Columbus and heading south to Mexico. How in the world was I going to get everything done by the first of March? With lots of help from Sheri and Albert, I could do it!

The first thing we did was move the RV from its rented storage space to my driveway in Grove City. Thus began the challenge of fitting everything I owned into a 32-foot RV. The biggest problem was the multiple boxes of family pictures and memorabilia. I had been the official family photographer at every event imaginable for the past 50-plus years. There was no time to sort through the pictures, so all of them would just have to go to Mexico. There was a lot of storage space on the RV, and I was determined it would all work out. It had to. I was counting the days. According to my calendar, when January ended, there were only twenty-eight days, exactly four weeks left until our departure.

Once again, on the morning of January 25th, Marshal Shadwick appeared at my front door for another interview. Most of his questions were the same as before. When he asked about the large recreational vehicle in the driveway, I informed him, "I'm moving with my daughter and her husband to Veracruz, Mexico, where my son-in-law has family." I explained that Sheri and Albert had bought a fifth-wheel trailer and had traveled to Columbus to help me get ready for the move. I told him I planned to return to Columbus to take my mother to Mexico by airplane, since she was not physically able to make such a long and strenuous trip, even in a house on wheels.

Do Me Twice
February 5, 2010

According to the newspaper, 30 inches of snow fell in Columbus during the month of February. It was the most snow ever recorded for that month. In addition to the snow, the temperature was brutally cold. Many days during the month, the temperature fell below zero.

Bobby and his wife made an unannounced visit to Columbus; it was quite a surprise. Out of the blue, he called to ask if Sheri, Albert and I could meet him for lunch at Appleby's Restaurant in Grove City. We wondered how he could afford the airfare for two, Arizona to Columbus, when he had been destitute for almost two years. He told the family he had no income since Becky disappeared, and he had been unsuccessful in finding suitable employment. I love Bobby, and had forgiven him for setting me up with the marshals during our taped phone conversation about Becky's manuscript. It was impossible to forget what he'd done to me, but regrets are only good for wallowing in. Nevertheless, we could hardly wait to see Bobby again. It had been a very long time, and we were anxious to meet his new wife. It was also a chance for me to get rid of a large box of Becky's things, discovered while cleaning out the house. I had planned to give the box to Bobby's father, who lives near Columbus, but putting it directly in Bobby's hands was even better. The box contained mostly framed pictures of Becky and Bobby and memorabilia-type items. Also in the box were two copies of Becky's manuscript. She had asked me to make certain that each of her two grandchildren were given a copy.

When I first saw Bobby at the restaurant, I hardly recognized him. The past two years, since his mother's disappearance, had really taken a toll on him. He was much thinner and looked about ten years older. I couldn't help feeling very sorry for him. He seemed so lost and abandoned. Being Becky's only child, he had been spoiled, pampered and provided with a luxurious lifestyle during his entire forty-plus years. Following the usual hugs and kisses, we had a really nice lunch together. Sheri, Albert and I talked mostly about our plans regarding our upcoming trip to Mexico in just a few more weeks. When it was time to go, I gave Bobby a big hug and kiss, reassuring him that I felt certain his mother was alive and well.

My last words to Bobby were, "You need to take better care of yourself and get on with your own life. Stop worrying about your mother. I'm certain you'll see her again one day. You'll have to come to Mexico and visit us when we get settled. I love you very much."

Much to my disappointment, I found out later that as soon as we left the restaurant, Bobby called Marshal Shadwick and reported to him everything that had been said during our entire time together. It also cleared up the mystery as to where the funds came from to purchase two airline tickets to Columbus.

I could not help but think of the very simple but oh so true adage, "Do me once, shame on you. Do me twice, shame on me!

Arrested!
February 12, 2010

The morning of February 12, I was arrested in my home by the U.S. Marshals and a SWAT team. After I was arrested and brought to the Franklin County Jail, I was left in a jail cell for most of the day, where I cried non-stop. I was not allowed to make a phone call or talk to anyone, and I was kept handcuffed and in ankle shackles.

"This is some kind of nightmare," I kept telling myself. Much later that afternoon, still in handcuffs and shackles, I was taken to a room divided by a glass wall. On the other side of the wall sat Marshal Shadwick. He slapped his hand, containing a piece of paper with something written on it, onto the glass right in front of my face. Scrawled on the torn piece of paper was the phrase, "lola221260@gmail.com." It was Becky's secret email address. I was shocked.

"How in the world," I asked myself, "did Marshal Shadwick find out about the email account Becky set up so we could communicate?"

Shadwick glared at me and said, "Are you ready to talk now?"

I looked at him with my red, swollen eyes and said, "I believe I need to speak to an attorney."

At that, Marshal Shadwick stormed out of the room, obviously very upset. I was taken back to the cell, where I remained for several more hours, crying ceaselessly. I felt as if my world had come to an end.

It was dusk when I was finally taken out of the Franklin County jail cell and driven thirty miles to the Delaware County Jail in Delaware, Ohio. I hadn't eaten anything all day, and I was beginning to feel nauseated. I still wasn't allowed to make a phone call or talk to anyone. I was about to begin the worst night of my entire life.

Upon arrival at Delaware County jail, two male officers finally removed my handcuffs and feet shackles. Corrections Officer Roxanne Himmler* was on duty at the registration desk where a large wall clock read 5:20p.m. After I answered a litany of routine, admission-type questions, she asked me to sign a document which she shoved in front of me. Since I had been crying all day, my contacts were causing my eyes to sting and my eyesight was very poor; everything was blurry. I explained to Officer Himmler that I could not see what she asked me to sign; I asked if I could have some eye drops. She became very angry and said, "If you don't sign it now, you'll have to wait right here until the next shift comes in at 10:00 p.m. when the nurse comes on duty." She was very rude and condescending towards me. Waiting five more hours in that uncomfortable chair did not sound possible to me in my state of exhaustion. So, even though I could barely see, I signed the paper reluctantly.

Finally, I was allowed to make "one brief phone call" per Officer Himmler. I could not wait to phone my daughter.

"Poor Sheri," I thought when she began talking.

She sounded even more distraught than I felt, but she was ecstatic to finally hear that I was alive, at least. We were both crying hard; we could scarcely speak. We had planned to get together around 10:00 a.m. that day. When Sheri arrived at the house at our agreed upon time, she found Marshal Shadwick and most of the SWAT team still there. She informed me they had ransacked the entire house, heaping what they did not want in a large pile in the center of each room. Sheri had talked with Marshal Shadwick, and she had signed documents which listed the items removed from the house. She shared her relief that I did not see how much they had torn the house apart. Somehow, Sheri also managed to make an appointment for the next day, Saturday, with an attorney that she found in the yellow pages. The dog and cats were fine, she assured me.

Since my daughter was not aware of my communications with Becky, she was shocked to hear what I had been accused of doing. She, more than anyone else, knew how terribly Becky treated me over the years; Sheri could not believe I would attempt to help Becky at the expense of my own well-being.

"I love you, Mom," Sheri said to me. "We'll get you out of there. In the meantime, you must be strong and take care of yourself. Okay?"

As Officer Himmler was motioning for me to get off the phone, I said, "I'll be all right, Honey. I love you, too."

I hung up, but I did not really believe that I was going to be okay.

At this point, still sobbing and in a daze, I was turned over to Officer Katherine Thompson*. She, at least, treated me like a human being; she led me to a room where I was instructed to take a shower and wash my hair. Then I was examined, head to toe, to make certain that I wasn't carrying any contraband into the jail. It was even colder in this jail than the one downtown. It was so frigid in the jail the officers wore their heavy uniforms and winter jackets. I had been freezing all day long. The temperatures outside had been hovering in the 20°s for the past week; inside, the jail did not feel much warmer. I wasn't allowed to keep any of my clothing. Instead, Officer Thompson handed me the standard jail outfit which consisted of an orange V-neck, short-sleeved cotton shirt and matching, straight-legged pants with an elastic waist. The outfit was much too large for me; which made the air feel even colder. According to procedure, I was not permitted to wear my own underwear or socks because they did not happen to be white. The two lightweight cotton garments, and a pair of orange canvas slippers, were all I was given to wear.

I found out later that you had to be an inmate for thirty days before you qualified for a white t-shirt. If you had cash with you – which I, unfortunately did not – you could put money into an account and purchase certain items from the commissary. To complicate the acquisition further, the money had to be in your account for three days before placing an order. Mondays were the only order days and Wednesdays, at midnight, were the delivery days. Inmates were required to get out of bed on Wednesdays at midnight in order to receive and sign for their commissary items. As the day of my arrest was a Friday, it would be almost two weeks before I could actually receive additional clothing or other personal items.

I was turned over to another female Corrections Officer, CO, who escorted me into yet another area of the jail. We stopped at a supply cabinet where I was given two ragged, cot-sized sheets, one cot-sized wool blanket, scratchy and full of holes, a miniature bath towel, only twice the size of a kitchen hand towel, and an "indigent package": one small bar of soap, two ounces of shampoo, one small comb, one toothbrush, half the normal size, and one very small tube of toothpaste.

We continued down several hallways until we finally arrived at an area called the housing area, comprised of individual cells and a communal "living area". After going through two heavy, metal, locked doors and a glass vestibule area, we entered a long narrow room with four very small tables attached to the left wall and enough seating for seven inmates. Above the tables, attached to the wall near the ceiling was a small television. Just beyond the tables, there was an area containing an open shower and toilet, separated only by a three-foot-tall metal partition. Located on a wall near the front was a telephone and built-in intercom box. Four separate cells were located on the right side of the room. The cell doors were metal, about six inches thick, with one small, heavy-duty glass window in the center. They were controlled electronically by officers from outside the cell area.

The officers' station could not be seen, or heard, from inside the cells; it was located in the front office at the opposite end of the building. A single camera, inside the housing area but outside the actual cells, provided the officers with the only view of what was pathetically referred to as the "living area". Unlike other inmate areas where COs were on duty twenty-four hours a day, the housing area was provided with an officer only a few hours during each eight-hour shift. The remainder of the time, communication between inmates and COs was only possible through the intercom system.

All four individual cell doors were open when the CO escorted me to my cell, number G10. There were no other inmates in this section. The actual jail cells were tiny, rectangular spaces, each containing a small, barred window set high in the cement block wall opposite the door. There was a metal cot attached to one wall and a small intercom box built-in to the opposite wall. Lastly, each cell was outfitted with one toilet and a small sink.

When the officer left me in G10, she turned on the television and said she would be back later to check on me. I was alone and miserable. My eyes were burning terribly, painful and dry from crying. The officer said I would have to wait until the nurse came on duty at 9:00 p.m. to get eye drops. It was dark outside now, pitch black outside the window in my cell. I decided to brush my teeth before collapsing from emotional exhaustion. I turned on the cold water in the lavatory, but then I could not turn it off; the sink filled up and began overflowing onto the floor. After a few tries on the intercom, someone from the front office finally answered. More than fifteen minutes went by before a repairman came to shut the water off. Luckily, the cement floors were slanted and the water flowed downhill into a large drain in the middle of the cell living area. The drain was covered by a grate, but I could still see the dirt foundation below it and a few bugs swimming around. I was moved to cell G9. By now, it was truly late.

Finally, the announcement came over the intercom that the night nurse had arrived with her cart full of medicine. To add further to my agony, the nurse said she could not give me eye drops until I had been to the head nurse's station. I begged her for some drops for my burning eyes, but she insisted that I fill out a form to be seen at the nurse's station first. I filled out the form. There would be no relief for my eyes until the following day, at least. In the meantime, the night nurse gave me two very small plastic cups in which to place my contact lenses. When I finally removed my contact lenses, it was incredibly painful; my eyes were very dry. The nurse could not give me any saline solution to put in the tiny cups, unfortunately. With no other choice, I was forced to put the contact lenses in plain water, potentially causing them permanent damage.

Back in my cell, unable to see clearly, all I wanted to do was lie down and try to get warm. I had never been so cold in my entire life. I wrapped toilet paper around my feet and wore my shoes to bed. Instead of using the tattered sheets to cover the worn out two-inch-thick mattress, I wrapped the sheets around my chest and legs. The rough wool blanket barely reached around my body. There were no pillows in jail. My eyes were shut, but I could not sleep. My mind was racing with thoughts of the most horrible day of my life and of just what tomorrow would bring.

All night long, the metal cell doors and metal doors leading into the cell area kept opening and shutting, making a loud, "Bang!" each time they opened and closed electronically. The night was filled with voices, people taking showers, a television blaring, a cacophony of noise. I was wrapped up like a caterpillar in a cocoon, warmer than I had been all day, and I did not move again until morning arrived.

Rude Awakening
February 13, 2010

Although I do not remember falling asleep, I must have dozed off briefly when the banging sound of all four cell doors opening at once startled me out of my cocoon. The overhead light was shining brightly, and it was still dark outside. A voice from the intercom speaker said, "Breakfast, ladies." As I sat on the side of the cot, still wrapped up in the meager bedclothes, my head was pounding. Each beat in my head was accompanied by a sharp pain. It was a major headache. The previous day was no nightmare. I really *was* in jail.

Although I did not have access to *The Columbus Dispatch* or any newspaper because they are not allowed in jail, I learned the February 13 front page of the "Metro and State" section contained the following: "NATIONAL CENTURY Sister was emailing fugitive, feds say. Women allegedly planned to meet soon in Mexico." The article reported that "The sister of the fugitive National Century founder had planned to move to Mexico to be with her by Valentine's Day, officials said. But yesterday, Linda Case, 66, of Grove City, was arrested at her home and jailed pending a detention hearing on Tuesday in federal court. Case, who was charged with obstruction of justice and lying to investigators, was accused of emailing her sister Rebecca S. Parrett regularly since 2008. Federal agents

intercepted the emails, which indicated that Parrett was
hiding in Mexico. Assistant U.S. Attorney Douglas W.
Squires, one of the prosecutors who handled the
National Century trials, said yesterday that he couldn't
discuss Case's arrest."

Another article, appearing in *Business Week*,
was entitled, "Sister of National Century Fugitive
Parrett Arrested." I did not see these articles until many
months later; I had more immediate priorities.

Except for cell G10 with the water problem, the
remaining two cells were filled with female prisoners
during the night. I found out later the housing area held
mostly federal inmates as opposed to county and state
inmates charged with lesser type crimes. Those inmates
were housed in the dormitory section and their length
of stay in the jail was usually much shorter than the
federal inmates.

The standard jail breakfast consisted of oatmeal,
a boiled egg or two, one slice of white bread with a
packet of jelly and small containers of milk and juice.
The breakfast menu did not ever vary, except for an
occasional potato patty. There was no coffee, no sugar,
no salt, no pepper, no butter, not ever. The only
drinking water available was from the sinks, and it was
cloudy in color and tasted terrible. That first morning, I
could not eat a bite.

"Thank goodness," I thought, "at least I'll be out
of here in a day or two."

Immediately following breakfast, everyone was
assigned their chores for the day. Assignations were
decided by the officer on duty and consisted of
sweeping or mopping the "living area", cleaning the
shower area, cleaning the communal toilet and lavatory,
cleaning tables and chairs, polishing glass windows,

wiping down walls, disinfecting the phone, basically cleaning everything in the entire, shared living area plus one's individual cell.

The morning nurse showed up around 10:00 a.m. She was different from the night nurse but still would not give eye drops to me until I had been seen at the nurse's station. I turned in the paperwork the night before, but no one seemed to know just how long it would be before I would get some relief for my burning eyes. This nurse was kind enough to provide me with two aspirin for my splitting headache, at least.

Even though I had been booked into jail the prior evening, it was afternoon and the telephone was still not set up with proper information in order for me to be able to make outgoing phone calls. In order to make outgoing calls, one had to have either a phone card, purchased from the commissary, or phone one's party collect. The marshals had confiscated my home land-line phone as well as my cell phone. Sheri had to manually authorize collect calls on her cell phone, which had a California phone number. It was late evening when the only jail phone in our cell area was finally set up for my use. After many attempts, I finally reached Sheri. Later, we realized we had accrued several hundred dollars' worth of fees for just a few calls since we were phoning her California number, long-distance, collect, but there was no other way for us to communicate directly.

Ultimately, the cost was immaterial. It was priceless for me simply to hear Sheri's voice. We both cried and tried to console each other. Sheri was much stronger than me. I honestly felt my life had come to an end, and I would die or have a nervous breakdown if I remained in jail much longer. Sheri told me a hearing had been set for Tuesday morning since Monday was a holiday, Presidents' Day. She hired an attorney, John Smith,* who she found via his advertisement in the yellow pages. He was coming to see me the next day, Sunday. Thankfully, he had agreed to bring a bag containing my eye glasses as well as some eye drops and saline solution.

Later that night, at approximately 9:30 p.m., an officer took me to a holding cell close to the front office. This cell was commonly known as the "Freezer" since it was almost as cold as one.

There were other inmates in the Freezer, all waiting to see the nurse. The waiting area was very small. Seating was a bench on one wall that seated four or five bodies, at most. A toilet and hand-washing sink were the only other items in the small room, with no partitions to accommodate privacy.

It was after midnight, almost three hours later, when an officer finally took me out of the Freezer and into the nurse's office. The nurse spent less than five minutes with me before giving me a tiny vial of eye drops. She informed me that someone from outside the jail would have to bring a new, unopened container of eye drops to the jail for my continued use. This same procedure was true for the saline solution used for cleaning my contact lens. It was required that these personal items be kept on the nurse's cart, and they were available to me only twice per day, when the nurse made her rounds.

"This kind of treatment is inhumane," I thought to myself.

I had never been in jail before, never even visited anyone in jail before. The conditions were worse than I could ever have imagined: no underwear, no properly warm clothing, nor any eye drops for my burning eyes. These were simple, basic necessities! All of the officers and staff seemed cruel and uncaring. After seeing the nurse, a different officer escorted me back to the Freezer where I remained until all the other inmates had been seen by the nurse. Only then did an officer accompany all of us back to our respective cells.

A scant few items, such as white socks and white underwear, were allowed to be brought to inmates from outside the jail. These items were required to be in new, unopened packages. Everything else had to be purchased through the commissary with monies put on your account by someone from the outside. Not all of the inmates had someone on the outside to put money on their account. Aside from an indigent package once a week, they simply had to do without.

Valentine's Day Behind Bars
February 14, 2010

It was Sunday afternoon when my attorney, Mr. Smith arrived. We were seated in a small room furnished only with a small table and two chairs. After the usual introductions, Mr. Smith handed me his business card. The front side contained his name, address and phone number. The back of the card contained an inscription reading "You have the right to remain silent. Anything you say can and will be used against you. *Miranda v. Arizona 384 U.S. 436 (1966).* DON'T SPEAK TO ANYONE, ESPECIALLY THE POLICE, WITHOUT CALLING ME FIRST!"

According to Smith, the right to remain silent was called my *Miranda Rights.*

"I've never heard this term before," I said. "At no time during any of my conversations with the marshals was I ever told that I had the right to remain silent. If I had been aware of that option, there is no way that I would be sitting in a jail right now!"

I felt certain that, if I had been told about my right to remain silent I would have known that I could simply answer, "I have nothing to say". That statement would not have been considered lying to the marshals. Thus, I might have avoided jail and this entire nightmare. To my knowledge, during all the days and months that followed, Smith never mentioned to the court, or anyone in my defense, that I had never been given my *Miranda Rights*. I felt this was a very significant piece of information that just got swept under the rug.

Attorney Smith did not respond; he changed the subject and gave me some very startling news. It turns out that Smith had actually been one of Becky's attorneys prior to her trial. I asked him why he had not remained her attorney.

"Becky and I disagreed as to whether or not she should plea bargain," he replied. "I told her she would possibly receive as little as four years in prison and would, most likely, be out in two years. Becky said she wasn't going to spend one day in prison for something she didn't do, however."

It did not seem right to me. I didn't want to be represented by an attorney who had previously represented Becky, especially one that had been dismissed by her! Wouldn't Smith be biased towards me? It seemed there was no choice but to keep him as my attorney, unfortunately. After all, Sheri had already hired Smith and paid a large retainer fee before legal representation could even begin. Was it a coincidence or did Smith deliberately keep that information from Sheri, so she wouldn't retain a different attorney to represent me?

Attorney Smith discussed my case and the evidence the government had against me. The evidence was copies of emails between Becky and me beginning around June 2009, after Attorney Riley violated my attorney/client privilege. Riley gave the marshals the email address and password Becky created. With that information, Smith explained, Marshal Shadwick obtained a search warrant, a pen register, and a "trap and trace" on the email account. Both commonly used in surveillance, a pen register is a device that records all numbers called from a given telephone, outgoing, or a program that performs similar tasks with internet communications; a "trap and trace" executes parallel functions for incoming calls and email. Marshal Shadwick continued to track Becky through our email communications and determined that she was somewhere in Mexico. I finally understood why my innocent and unrelated plans to relocate to Mexico seemed so suspicious to him.

Becky never told me where she was, and I never asked. I did not want to know where she was. I suspected she might be in Mexico or another country nearby like Costa Rica or Nicaragua, but I never knew for sure. On several occasions, Becky mentioned she had moved again, but she never mentioned where. In my mind, I was simply communicating with Becky, which was not against the law. Until my arrest, I had no idea the consequences of my actions could land me in jail or worse, prison.

Before departing that day, Attorney Smith gave me a yellow legal pad. He asked me to write down everything I could think of that might help with my defense. He said he would see me on Tuesday morning prior to the Preliminary Hearing. The purpose of the Preliminary Hearing is to determine whether the defendant, me, should stand trial or be released.

The only writing utensils allowed in jail were free, rubber-type pencils and tiny little pencils, like those used for keeping golf scores, which could only be purchased from the commissary. I borrowed a tiny pencil from another inmate and tried to begin writing as soon as I returned to my cell. My mind was a blank. I was still in a fog and couldn't believe this was happening to me. I had never felt so helpless and so hopeless in my entire life; all I could do was cry. It was

Valentine's Day. I was supposed to be having a happy family dinner with my mother, Sheri and Albert. I began to cry and remembered, "Life is not what it is supposed to be, it is what it is."

Court Appearance
February 16, 2010

I spent Presidents' Day, February 15, in jail writing down everything that happened between Becky and me over the previous eight years. The yellow pad was completely full, and there was still much more to tell.

The next morning, at 5:00 a.m., I was awakened by a female officer and told to get dressed. The officer said she would be back for me in five minutes. Since I had slept in my clothes in order to keep warm, all I needed to do was to remove the toilet paper from my shoes and the sheets from around my body. Beginning so early in the morning was standard procedure for federal inmates when they had to be present for a hearing at the federal building in downtown Columbus.

When the officer returned, she took me up front and put me in the Freezer, where I remained until 7:30 a.m. Two male police officers handcuffed me, put shackles around my ankles, and escorted me outside to the police car. It was so bitterly cold my body was shaking all over. Orange jackets were available for inmates, but I did not know that at the time, and the officers did not care enough to offer me one.

"Animals are treated better than this," I thought.

There were two male inmates, handcuffed and shackled, who were also scheduled for a federal hearing that day. I was seated between them in the back seat.

After a while, one of the officers turned up the car heater. For the first time in days, my body began to thaw out.

When we arrived downtown I was put into another cell, separate from the male inmates, where I remained until approximately 9:00 a.m. I noticed the federal officers were all males. One of them escorted me to a small room containing two seats, one on each side of a glass partition. Attorney Smith was seated on the opposite side. We talked about my case until it was time for my hearing, which was scheduled for 9:30 a.m.

The courtroom was cold and intimidating. Sheri was seated in the courtroom, but I was not allowed to talk to her or give her a hug. She appeared tired and frightened. With no prior convictions of any kind, I felt confident my attorney would get me released on bond or on my own recognizance. After all, even suspected murderers get out on bond sometimes. When the judge entered the room, however, my chances for being released flew out the window. It was Judge Algenon L. Marbley, the same trial judge who had presided over the National Century case, the same judge who released Becky following her trial and conviction. He looked at me with eyes that pierced right through me. Becky had embarrassed him by fleeing and becoming a wanted fugitive. At that moment, I knew he was not about to let me go anywhere.

There was no actual hearing scheduled for today, just an appearance before the judge. Later, I understood that the hearing's outcome had been decided long before I ever arrived. My attorney had already sent a *Waiver of Preliminary Hearing and Detention Hearing* to the court and to the judge. He did this without discussing it with me at all. Attorney Smith was certain the judge was going to deny my release from jail, no matter what, so there was no point in having an actual hearing. Today was simply a formality.

In the minds of the judge, the marshals, even my own attorney, Becky was a fugitive, and therefore, I was a flight risk, too, and should be detained in jail. But, there was no way I should have been considered a flight risk! The marshals had confiscated my passport, my automobile and RV titles, all my liquid assets including cash. I had nothing left. How could I possibly go anywhere even if I wanted to? How could I, even remotely, be considered a flight risk? I was devastated! I began to cry again. As they escorted me from the courtroom, I glanced at Sheri; she was crying too. I put my shackled hands on my heart and hoped that my eyes revealed how much I loved and appreciated her. It was the only way I was allowed to communicate with my daughter.

Attorney Smith and I were granted a few minutes together before the officers took me back to the cell.

"Mr. Smith, what do we have to do to get a different judge?" I requested. "There is no way I will be treated fairly by the same judge who let Becky get away. It seems to me that he should recuse himself from being my judge."

"If we ask for a different judge and our request is denied, it will be even harder for you," he replied.

"In other words," I thought to myself, "I am really screwed! With *this* judge and Mr. Smith as my attorney, I don't stand a chance. My life is over!"

It was late evening when the police officers took me from the federal courtroom holding cell to the police car and back to Delaware County Jail. Also in the vehicle were several other male inmates.

Apparently, the officers made only one trip per day to transport all Federal inmates who were scheduled for a hearing on the same day.

Upon arrival back at Delaware County Jail, my handcuffs and shackles were removed and I was placed back in the Freezer for several more hours before an officer arrived to escort me back to my cell. I felt the Freezer was effectively a torture chamber; there was absolutely no other reason for leaving inmates in that cell for hours on end with no way to keep warm.

The following day, an article appeared in *The Columbus Dispatch.* The headline read, "Sister of National Century fugitive to stay in jail for now." The article reported the following:

"A Grove City woman accused of lying to investigators about her fugitive sister remained in jail yesterday after waiving a federal court hearing to challenge her detention.

The attorney for Linda Case said he needed more time to prepare arguments to support her release from custody while awaiting trial. John E. Smith said he will ask for the hearing to be rescheduled soon.

Case, 66, is the sister of Rebecca Parrett. The National Century founder fled the country after a federal jury in March 2008 convicted her of wire and securities fraud and other crimes related to the collapse of the health-care financing company.

Federal agents arrested Case on Friday and charged her with obstruction of justice and making false statements to law enforcement after investigators intercepted email communications between her and Parrett. The emails showed that Case, who told investigators that she didn't know where they could find her sister, was planning to meet Parrett in Mexico.

Parrett, 61, was sentenced last year in absentia to 25 years in prison. Each charge filed against Case is punishable by up to five years in prison."

Secrecy and Despair
February 18 - 25, 2010

Over the next seven, lonely days in jail, I felt myself fading away, disappearing from any semblance of life I had ever known. I had absolutely no control over anything that happened inside or outside my jail cell. Every day was the same. I spent every day thinking, remembering, writing, and racking my brain to think of anything, no matter how small that could possibly help me out of this nightmare. The only thing that kept me from falling apart completely was my daily phone conversation with Sheri.

Sheri was unbelievable! She and Albert moved into the big house in Grove City to take care of Sonny Boy, my dog, and the seven cats, my four and my mother's three. Sheri began to sort through my computer documents and emails, which were still on my computer from the year 2003, to assist in my defense. She prepared a timeline from 1998 to the present and a four-page document entitled "Background." She made hundreds of copies of pertinent information which proved, without a doubt, that our plans to go to Mexico had begun in 2003 and had absolutely nothing to do with my sister, Becky, Rebecca Parrett. Sheri gave this enormous amount of important information to Attorney Smith.

On February 22, an article appeared in *The Columbus Dispatch*. The headline read, "Fugitives often fall to lure of family. National Century exec on well-worn path, experts say."

The article was all about Becky except for one part. It said Harvey Handler, a local bail bondsman for 38 years, "thinks the arrest of Parrett's sister was a move calculated to pressure Parrett to turn herself in. 'They're using a very strong tactic,' he said. 'I'd say the government finally got their break.'"

If the government thought Becky would turn herself in to get me off the hook, they were sadly mistaken. She did not care about me. If she did, she never would have put me in jeopardy by contacting me to begin with.

On February 24, I was awakened at 5:00 a.m. and, once again, taken to the federal building in downtown Columbus. The procedure was the same as before, except, this time I was the only passenger in the police vehicle. I was taken to a small room where Marshal Shadwick and Attorney Smith were waiting, along with the Prosecuting Attorney, Doug Squires. I was interrogated for several hours, in tears most of the time.

"Your life will never be the same again," Squires said to me, pointedly. The meeting was not scheduled on any roster or docket; it was kept confidential from my family and, especially, the news media. By the end of the meeting, the Prosecuting Attorney agreed to charge me with *One Count of False Statements* in exchange for a *Plea Agreement*. Even though the formal charge against me stated that I "denied knowing that Parrett was residing in the country of Mexico," (rather than the truth which was I did not know where she was) I was so scared and so vulnerable that I signed the *Plea Agreement* anyway. I had lied to Marshal Shadwick about communicating with Becky, but I never knew her location. By pleading guilty and signing the *Plea Agreement*, an indictment and trial would no longer be necessary.

An *Information* hearing before the judge was scheduled for two days later. The *Plea Agreement* and all other official court documents were marked, "Sealed". On February 25, upon motion of the government, Magistrate Judge Kemp signed an Order that the *Information, Plea Agreement* and future (Linda) Case filings be sealed. Sealing is the process used by courts to keep some proceedings and records confidential. I wondered why my case was increasingly being made confidential. Was the bail bondsman correct? Did they really think Becky would give herself up in order to help me? I knew I would rot in jail before Becky would do anything like that for me!

Jail Bait
February 26, 2010

My day began with great anticipation that today would be the day when this nightmare would end. I gave the marshals a complete and true accounting of everything I had done since Becky first contacted me. What more could I do? Surely, something would be decided today. Over and over, an old mantra kept going through my mind, "Everything terrible has a termination point. You will get through it."

I was already awake when the loud thunder of my cell door opened and the CO announced it was time for me to get up for the Information Hearing. Thus began the court day routine of being awakened at 5:00 a.m., followed by a couple of hours in the Freezer. The male police officers arrived and, once again with handcuffs and feet shackled, we traveled downtown where I was placed into another holding cell until time for the hearing. Except for a brief time in the holding cell, my handcuffs and feet shackles remained in place, even in the courtroom. It was very difficult to walk with shackles on. I was afraid of tripping or falling and breaking a bone or worse. The temperature outside remained in the low twenties during the day. The wind was blowing which made the day even colder than usual. Still, no one cared enough to even offer me a jacket, and I still did not know of their existence.

There were very few people in the courtroom. For whatever reason, the government wanted my case to remain confidential. My attorney and I stood in front of the judge who read the government's charge against me, *Count One, False Statements.* He also read the contents of the *Plea Agreement.* I was extremely nervous and noticeably shaking. The judge was a powerful person. It was obvious to me, that he didn't like me one bit. As he was reading the documents, he kept asking me if I understood. I replied affirmatively even though I had no idea of what was actually happening to me. One thing I did understand was that the government was going to keep me behind bars until my sentencing date, which was yet to be determined. They insisted that I remained a flight risk. Following the devastating realization that I was going to remain in jail until sentencing, tears began running down my face again.

"What was I to do?" All I could seem to do was cry. "If tears are considered 'healing water,' why didn't I feel better after days and days of crying my eyes out?"

Before being escorted back to the cell, Attorney Smith and I met with Teri Adkins,* United States Probation Officer and Sentencing Guidelines Specialist. The purpose of the interview was to gather information, so Ms. Adkins could prepare a *Pre-sentence Investigation Report* and *Sentencing Recommendation* for the judge. The interview lasted over two hours. A few days later, I received a letter from my attorney explaining the court mandated Adkins to complete her report and deliver a copy to my attorney via certified mail by April 2, 2010. Upon receipt, Attorney Smith and I were to review the report and communicate any objections to Adkins no later than April 19, 2010, so that any objections could be resolved informally. The final *Presentence Investigation Report* had to be sent to the Court and Attorney Smith by May 10. That date was forty-one days away. Forty-one more days that I would definitely remain in jail!

"I'll never make it!" My heart was pounding rapidly and it felt like someone had just punched a hole in my chest. As my body became weak, I bent over and began to vomit.

Now, finally, the writing was on the wall. The government was planning to keep me in jail as long as they possibly could by calling me a "flight risk." They thought that Becky would certainly come to my rescue. It was clear; they were using me as bait in hopes of getting some kind of a reaction from Becky. What a joke that was. But, I wasn't laughing. I knew Becky all too well.

It was really late when I returned to my cell in Delaware County Jail. I went straight to bed and cried myself to sleep.

Life Behind Bars
March 2010

March came in like a lion with more snow and more icy cold temperatures. The only good thing about my jail cell was the fact that it had a window. Through the bars, I could see a railroad track, lots of snow-covered trees, a tall barbed-wire fence and an occasional squirrel or bird. Once or twice a day, a train would roar by. Oh, how I longed to have my life back.

Except for daily meals and chores, there was nothing to do, no exercise programs, no rehabilitation programs, just lots of time to think. There was too much time to dwell on the negative aspects of my current situation. I had always been a positive and happy person, so I decided to stop feeling sorry for myself and to earnestly try to think only positive thoughts.

"Everything happens for a reason," I told myself. Since it looked as though I would remain in jail for weeks, possibly even months, I sincerely decided to bring something good out of this horrible nightmare I had gotten myself into.

"After all," I said to myself, "Life is not about waiting for the storm to pass, it's about learning how to dance in the rain!"

Following breakfast and morning chores, most of the inmates went back to bed. Being a morning person, I began exercising for at least an hour every morning; I watched *The Dr. Oz Show* and the *Rachel Ray Show,* where I obtained many interesting recipes. I would kid the other inmates whom I called girls, and say, "When I get out of jail, I'm going to publish a recipe book called *Linda's Jailhouse Recipes*." That always gave everyone a good laugh.

At roughly 11:00 a.m., the girls would start getting out of bed because it was time for lunch. Lunches and dinners were always the same types of food, mostly heavy starches (noodle casseroles, potatoes), some type of meat (which I never ate), a vegetable (which I always ate) and a dessert (flavored gelatin, pudding or an occasional brownie). After meals, we were required to dump our food trays into a large trash can. Some of the noodle casseroles were so starchy that they stuck to the tray even after pounding against the side of the metal trash can. After a while, I learned I could trade everything else on my plate in exchange for extra servings of vegetables or potatoes. It was not unusual for me to end up with three or four helpings of vegetables, especially peas, and nothing else.

We ate in the "living area" just outside our cells; there were two manhole-like floor drains, with only grates for covers, located right next to the eating area. This was where the daily mop water was dumped; it also acted as an overflow drain. Sometimes, the odor was so bad I totally lost my appetite. Once in a while, the drain would back up into the living/eating area and it would become necessary to evacuate everyone into a holding cell until the problem was fixed and the floor was dry. Most of the inmates gained weight. I lost over twenty pounds.

Soon after lunch, all inmates were required to go into their individual cells to be locked down. No movement was permitted during lockdown except for restroom use. During this time period, I usually read a book or just rested. When lockdown was over, it was almost time for dinner. After-dinner entertainment consisted of television, puzzles, books, card games or board games. A Correction Officer's presence was required to turn the television on or to change the channel. The bookcase, puzzles and games were physically located outside the living area. A CO escort was required in order to go outside the area to get a new book or game. Sometimes, we would have to wait hours before an officer would appear again. All supplies, even toilet paper, were located outside and could only be replenished when a CO was present.

I read tons of books and went to bed early, even before the night lockdown which began at 9:30 p.m. and lasted two hours. Every night, the cell doors opened again at 11:30 p.m., for one hour only. Almost everyone else would get back up and watch television or play games and make lots of noise before being locked down again at 12:30 a.m., for the remainder of the night; I did not join them. After the final lockdown, the loud cell doors would open and shut all night long with trustees, long-term inmates who have special privileges, coming in and out to take showers. It was impossible to sleep through the night without being awakened.

Every Thursday night, at midnight, all inmates had to get out of bed to complete assigned chores. I never understood the reasoning behind that rule; it seemed to be just another kind of torture, like the Freezer.

Commissary orders, placed on Mondays, were delivered on Wednesday nights at about midnight. Inmates were required to get out of bed to sign for their orders. It was always hard for me to get back to sleep.

The highlight of my evening was always my telephone conversation with Sheri. She was always so positive and genuinely concerned about my health and well-being while in jail, especially at my age.

I was the oldest female in the jail, by far. Most inmates were in their 20s and 30s, married or not with small children, and charged with drug use, drug dealing or both. It was utterly shocking. Many of the girls' entire lives revolved around being in and out of jail and/or prisons. They told me when they got out of jail, they had no place else to go except right back to the same environment, drugs, and friends who were also on drugs.

I will never forget Sharon, a young, beautiful blonde girl awaiting sentencing on drug related charges. She knew she was definitely going to prison. In the meantime, she was allowed to go home for thirty days to make arrangements for her pre-teen daughter and elderly father. Before she left jail, crying, she gave me a hug and said, "Linda, I'm scared to death that I'm going to relapse." A few days later, she was found dead with drug needles still stuck in her legs. I cried when I heard the news. What a waste of life. It made absolutely no sense to me.

The housing area cells began overflowing with inmates. Four federal inmates had been brought in from the Franklin County jail; there were now eight inmates in four cells. Since each cell was barely big enough for one person and contained only one bunk bed, the new inmates had to sleep on very thin mattresses on the floor. My cellmate was a Hispanic girl named Haydee.

She was really sweet, with a husband and young daughter at home; we became friends. Haydee was born in Mexico, but had been in the U.S. for more than ten years. She was here illegally and had just recently been arrested for the first time; her daughter and husband were both citizens. She cried a lot, afraid she was going to be deported. After a few weeks, Haydee was released on house arrest for eight months.

Another young inmate, Sabrina, 19 years old, became very attached to me. She was younger than some of my grandchildren. Her cell was next to mine; she was very tiny, pretty with long blonde hair, and her arms were black and blue, covered with needle marks. Most of her family members were drug addicts and had been in and out of prison. We talked often, and I gave her a lot of my food. I never saw such a tiny person eat so much food. Sabrina had been in jail before. Basically, she had no place to go when she got out except back to the same drug-infested environment. Her brother was currently in prison, and her mother had recently been sentenced to ten years in prison. The stories she shared with me about her life were unbelievable and very sad.

March Madness
March 19 - 31, 2010

O n March 19, 2010, I decided to write a letter to Judge Marbley and plead for my release. Sheri continued to work with Attorney Smith and Marshal Shadwick. She located and copied birth certificates, marriage licenses, divorce decrees, OSU diploma, family records, work history, addresses, income tax returns, vehicle titles, homeowner information and lots of additional information, all required for completion of the *Presentence Investigation Report.*

On March 23, the *Confidential Initial Presentence Investigation Report* and *Sentencing Recommendation* were completed by Teri Adkins and a copy was mailed to me from Attorney Smith's office. The *Investigation Report* contained 99 paragraphs of information that had to be discussed with Attorney Smith and, if needed, objections had to be communicated to Adkins and resolved, informally, no later than April 19, 2010. The final two pages of the report contained Adkins's initial *Sentencing Recommendation* which was thirty-six months in prison, two years supervised release and $100 special assessment.

Immediately after reading the sentence recommendation, my body began to shake all over; my heart began to beat rapidly and my head felt like it was filled with cotton. I began crying hysterically; I thought I was dying of a heart attack or stroke. In reality, I was having a full-blown anxiety attack for the first time in my life. I had heard the term, but I had never experienced one before. The nurse came quickly. She did not give me any medication, but I was moved to another area where I was monitored by the nurse until the out of control crying stopped and the other symptoms disappeared.

Meanwhile, my daughter continued to fight for my release. On March 29, Teri Adkins phoned Sheri for additional information. On March 30, Sheri wrote a four-page letter to Adkins on my behalf. On March 31, Sheri wrote a four-page letter to Judge Marbley on my behalf.

Along Came a Spider
April 2010

Young Sabrina was transferred near the first of the month to Maryhaven, a rehabilitation center in Columbus, after being sentenced. A few days later, a new inmate named Nancy was moved from another housing area into Sabrina's old cell, next door to me. Nancy shared the cell with Nadine whose nickname was "New York." Nadine was awaiting sentencing for drug dealing; she was looking at ten, or more, years in prison.

Nancy was an aggressive, loud, trouble-maker, a Hispanic woman who hated white girls. Several times, she mouthed-off to the COs, after which we would all get punished by being locked in our cells for the remainder of the day, or the television would be turned off. After a while, she began picking on me, the only white woman among the seven inmates. I became really frightened of her; she acted like a crazy person. Since I got along well with the other five inmates, I decided to fill out a form to request that Nancy be moved out of our area.

A couple nights later, a little past midnight, I was awakened by the loud sound of my cell door opening. Two Corrections Officers, one male and one female, came into my cell and one of them said, "Pack up your stuff, Case." I was so scared. I was afraid I had done something wrong.

"What on earth did I do? Where are you taking me?" I began to cry.

Finally, the female officer said, "Wrap your stuff up in your sheets and blanket. We're moving you to the dorm."

"But, why?" I asked. "I don't want to move."

"It's not up to you. Just pack up your shit," the male officer growled.

After a short walk down some unfamiliar hallways, the officers unlocked a metal door which led into a large, open area divided down the middle by a cement wall about six feet high. Another CO was seated at a desk, just inside the door, in the front of the room. On the right side of the wall were twenty-four bunk beds where twenty-three inmates were sleeping. The clock on the wall said it was now 1:40 a.m. After signing me in, the female officer took me to my new space and said, "Make your bed, then get in it."

I was thankful it was a bottom bunk, at least. It was hard to see in the dim night light, but when I finally got my bed made and got back under the covers, I became hysterical again and continued to cry uncontrollably. I could not stop myself. I felt like I was being punished for something, but I did not know what. My head was under the covers; it began to feel as if it was going to explode. I imagined I must be having a nervous breakdown. A few minutes later, someone began to call my name and pull the tear-soaked covers away from my face. It was the nurse. She took me up front and began taking my vital signs. She explained that if I did not calm down I would be put in what she called a "pickle suit" and moved to isolation. That sounded pretty horrible. The nurse was especially nice to me; she stayed with me until my heart rate was stable, my blood pressure was normal, my headache was gone, and my crying had stopped. Her diagnosis was another anxiety attack. When I was finally back in bed, I prayed I would remain physically healthy and that my 66-year-old body would be able to continue to endure such unbelievably harsh emotional experiences. The magnitude of my heart-wrenching pain was second only to what I felt when my son died.

To my surprise, it was actually quiet in the dormitory. There were no electronic metal doors loudly opening and closing all night long. The night's ordeal had totally wiped me out. I remember consciously taking a few deep breaths through my nose before actually passing into a deep sleep.

The following morning, I was awakened when the bright, overhead lights came on. A voice said, "Everyone up for breakfast. Don't forget to make your beds first." Since I always slept in all my clothes, including shoes, all I had to do was force myself to put one foot in front of the other in order to begin another day in hell.

The dorm was one large open area with a cement wall separating the bunk beds from the eating area. The ceilings were high but there were no more than three small windows on the bunk side near the top of the wall. A very small minority of inmates could see out the windows if they were lucky enough to have a top bunk near one of the three undersized windows. There was a small, open office in the front of the room, just a desk and a file cabinet for the COs who were on duty in the dormitory twenty-four hours a day, seven days a week. If I stood on my toes, I could see over the dorm wall into the eating area where there were six, round, cement tables with four benches each bolted to the floor. A single television was mounted on the wall, and two wall telephones; there was also a bookcase full of books, cards and games open to everyone in the dorm at all times, unlike the "housing area" where I had spent the past two months. The only communal bathroom was also on the eating side of the big room. Through an open doorway, there was one shower, two toilets and two small sinks for 24 inmates to share, no doors.

Most of the inmates from the "housing area" insisted that the dormitory was much worse than the "housing area". After just a few days in the dorm, I totally disagreed. I liked having a CO continuously on duty. I truly appreciated the relative freedom of access to entertainment and, I especially valued the quiet nights. Finally, after two months in jail, I was able to get some much needed rest and sleep.

Daily routines in the dorm were the same as in the "housing area" as far as assigned chores, meal times and lockdown times. After the morning chores, when everyone else went back to bed, I continued my morning regimen of exercise and television shows. Most of the dorm inmates were not charged with federal crimes. Some would come in on Friday and Saturday nights, go before the Delaware County Court on Monday morning, and get released. Some were awaiting sentencing, headed to the State prison in Marysville.

Easter Behind Bars
April 4, 2010

Meanwhile, my daughter Sheri was having her own bouts with anxiety and depression at home in Grove City. For almost two months now she had been accomplishing small miracles on a daily basis. In my absence, she was taking care of everything and everyone. She cooperated with the attorneys and the marshals by doing hours of research and providing them with hundreds of pieces of evidence on my behalf. Still, nothing seemed to be happening; her mother was still behind bars after two months.

Easter arrived early this year, April 4, and Sheri was feeling pretty defeated the morning of Easter Sunday. She remembered a scene from our favorite Christmas movie, *It's a Wonderful Life*. When main character, George Bailey, was in trouble, his wife Mary reached out to family and friends for help. That scene inspired Sheri to sit down and write a letter to family and friends asking for help.

After an explanation of the situation, her letter said,

My mother's lawyer seems to think that personal letters to the judge will help my mother's case tremendously. That's where you come in. If you have anything kind to say about my mother, and her relationship with you, can you please write a letter to the judge and send it to me? I will give all the letters to her lawyer, and he will pass them on to the judge to review before my mother's sentencing.

Over the next few weeks, letters to the judge, as well as cards, letters and phone calls to Sheri began pouring in. I, too, began receiving lots of mail as Sheri had also included my jail address in her letter in case anyone wanted to contact me directly.

On April 21, Attorney Smith came to the jail to review our objections to the *Pre-Sentence Investigation (PSI) Report.*

April 29, I received a letter from Attorney Smith stating that he and the U.S. Attorney had tried to "get an informal status conference with the judge, but given the judge's schedule, we have been unable to schedule it. We, therefore, yesterday prepared a *Request for Detention Hearing Pending Sentencing,* a *Motion to File Request for Detention Hearing Pending Sentencing Under Seal,* and proposed *Entry.*" Smith's letter continued, "I was in touch with the Judge's Bailiff late in the day and they are out, so we have filed electronically today."

This all boiled down to a request to the judge to release me from jail until sentencing. The *Request* quoted a statute which states, in part,

A person subject to detention, and who meets the conditions of release, may be ordered released, under appropriate conditions, by the judicial officer, if it is clearly shown that there are exceptional reasons why such person's detention would not be appropriate.

The *Request* also stated,

In this case, there is clear and convincing evidence that Ms. Case will not flee and poses no danger to the safety of any other person or the community if released.

On April 30th, a *Detention Hearing,* under *Sealed Notice,* was set for May 3, 2010 at 9:00a.m.

Considering all the information Sheri and I had provided to the Court and Attorney Smith, coupled with all the letters written to the judge on my behalf, I was very optimistic that I was finally going to be released from jail until my sentencing court date.

The Awful Truth
May 2010

In jail, I had plenty of time for self-reflection; I arrived at some important insights concerning the events that led up to my incarceration. I ultimately came to the realization that thus far I had judged myself by my intentions, while the world, at least the judicial system, was judging me by my actions. The choices we make define us. My choices were not made with evil intentions, but rather to fulfill a promise to my brother, Dan, on his death bed; I agreed to take care of my mother and Becky in his absence. Later, I chose to maintain contact with Becky in order to keep my mother mentally and emotionally stable, possibly even alive, by regularly proving to her that her daughter was alive and well. My intentions were honorable. My actions were not. Actions have consequences. In retrospect, I could see some of my choices were wrong, and the effects of my decisions would linger long past the events. I have always prided myself in trying to "do the right thing." But, sometimes the right thing is not a clear and straightforward decision.

This life lesson, like others before it, sneakily took me by surprise. I took some small comfort in knowing that at least I had tried to make the right choice based on my good intentions. To quote Charles Barnard, "To try and fail is at least to learn; to fail to try is to suffer the inestimable loss of what might have been."

I definitely learned a critical lesson in all of this concerning action versus intention.

Freedom Denied
May 3, 2010

Sleep eluded me most of the night May 3rd; I was thinking of my impending day in court which would decide my release from detention. I prayed, meditated and visualized my release. Awake at 4:00 a.m., I brushed my teeth, put in my contact lenses, and tried breathing exercises in an attempt to lower my stress level. At 5:30 a.m., the CO escorted me to the Freezer for the usual two hours of frigid torture. Finally, handcuffed and shackled, I was on my way to the Federal Building in downtown Columbus.

It was a gorgeous day, seventy-five degrees, sunny and simply beautiful! Flowers were blooming; large, white, puffy clouds contrasted with the deep blue sky. I was soaking it all in. I felt sad to be missing all these beautiful days while locked inside cement walls. Only during trips to the courthouse was I able to breathe fresh air. The Delaware County Jail Rules regarding recreation stated, "Every opportunity will be taken to allow inmates to take part in recreational activities. At least one hour, five days per week is recommended. Outdoor recreation will be held, weather permitting."

This never happened. Recreation was not ever provided, outside or inside, period. I had been locked up for eighty-one days with no recreation of any kind.

Attorney Smith and Sheri were already in the Courtroom when I arrived. Sheri looked so pretty! I wanted so badly just to touch her, to give her a big hug, but that was not allowed. Since the hearing was sealed, there were very few people allowed in the courtroom, and no media.

After the judge entered the courtroom, the customary opening remarks were made; then I was asked by the court, "Please come forward, have a seat and be sworn." Attorney Smith asked me some general questions.

Then, he asked me to tell the court, "Why, number one, are you not a risk to leave if you were released? Number two, why are you not a risk to anyone in the community if you were to leave, just in your own words?"

I was incredibly nervous, but somehow managed to read my written statement to the court. The judge was not listening. He glared at me and began asking me questions, most of which were centered around whether or not I knew for certain that Becky was in Mexico.

Several times, I repeated the same statement, "I suspected that Becky was in Mexico, but I never knew for sure. She never volunteered that information and I never asked."

Judge Marbley's tone was very vindictive towards me. Several times he called me by my sister's last name, "Ms. Parrett." It was obvious to me that he was projecting his frustrations with Becky onto me. I was never more relieved than when I heard the words, "Ms. Case, thank you very much. You may step down." I felt like I had just been interrogated for allegedly committing a murder, not for telling a lie.

Next, Sheri was allowed to read a statement to the court that she had prepared on my behalf.

"I know my mom has disappointed you. I know she lied. We all make mistakes. My mom made a big one. But it is not one that is unrecoverable or unforgiveable. My mom has been in jail for three months. She has fully cooperated with everyone. She has said she is sorry, and, once she is able to, she will do everything she can for the rest of her life to make this right for all of us. I forgive her and believe that she will. If I can give my mom another chance, surely you can, too?

"In the spirit of Mother's Day, I respectfully ask that my mom be allowed to return home to do what she does best, be a loving mom and a caring daughter."

I was never more proud of her than at that moment.

Another attempt was then made by my attorney to convince the court that I was "definitely **not** a flight risk and should be released until sentencing." Part of Attorney Smith's argument was as follows:

"Your Honor, I think objectively that she has no resources to go anywhere. She would welcome the opportunity to be under house arrest with electronic monitoring, whatever the Court feels is necessary. She's willing to pledge what little she has. They have her titles to her cars and everything else. I think her daughter and son-in-law would be willing to do the same, whatever arrangements might be needed, checking in daily, checking in hourly, whatever would be needed. She's willing to do that to be back home until sentencing, and spend some time, quality time, hopefully, with her mother for Mother's Day and her mother's eighty-sixth birthday. I guess for all of those reasons, Your Honor, I've presented many cases for people to be released pending sentencing or resolution of their case, and I have no one that I would better bet on than Linda Case, would honor every request and every restriction that the Court might want on her, and she would follow through with that. Thank you."

The judge then stated, "I'm going to take a recess. I'm going to stand in recess until 10:30 a.m., at which time I'll come back and announce my decision."

The thirty minute recess seemed like hours. At last, the judge appeared back in the courtroom with his decision. My stomach was in knots. Although Attorney Smith had substantiated and compelling arguments for my release, the judge flatly said, "Detention is **not** appropriate." I really got my hopes up here. He cited all except one argument, all in favor of release; then, referring to the Code book again, he cited three arguments which backed up his first statement that it was NOT appropriate for me to be detained. He continued reading from the Code book as he said, "As I point out, I don't believe that there are factors here which establish by clear and convincing evidence that Ms. Case would not be a flight risk. So, the Court denies the motion for release pending sentencing."

The judge seemed so personally vengeful toward me. As I stood before him, my body became numb. All I could think about was how I was going to miss what would probably be my mother's last Mother's Day, and her eighty-sixth birthday, both just a few days away. What on earth had I done to deserve such cruel and unusual punishment? Even some murderers are released until sentencing. My crime was only telling a lie! Did the punishment really fit the crime?

A great sadness slowly tightened around my chest and heart like the crushing coils of a boa constrictor. How fragile, quick and unpredictable life is. Surprisingly, tears did not come this time; perhaps the reservoir was dry. I felt like a zombie as I was led out of the courtroom. I would be taken back to jail until sentencing, possibly weeks or even months away. At that moment, I was convinced I was not going to make it, that my life was over.

Why was the judge being so unreasonable over a temporary release for me? Was he guilty of what Marilynne Robinson wrote about in her book, *The Death of Alex, Essays on Modern Thought 1998*?

"We routinely disqualify testimony that would plead for extenuation. That is, we are so persuaded of the rightness of our judgment as to invalidate evidence that does not confirm us in it. Nothing that deserves to be called truth could ever be arrived at by such means."

These are dark times for our system of criminal justice. Recent verdicts in so-called high-profile cases have led to the broadly held conclusion that there is justice in this country only for those whose wealth or celebrity can buy it for them. I had neither.

FBI Offers Reward
May 6, 2010

T   *he Columbus Dispatch* reported the following on May 6, 2010, "Reward set for fugitive executive in $1.9 billion fraud, FBI hopes $10,000 will lead to woman convicted of fraud." The article stated, "The FBI is offering a reward of as much $10,000 for help in capturing fugitive Rebecca S. Parrett, according to Special Agent Harry W. Trombitas. Based on emails between Parrett and her sister, Linda L. Case of Grove City, federal agents believe that Parrett is in Mexico.

Since we didn't have newspapers in jail, I learned of the reward the following morning when the CO brought the newspaper article for me to read. At this point, I didn't care about Becky. I didn't care about a reward. Just three days earlier, my freedom had once again been denied. I was depressed, sick and tired of the judicial system using me as jail bait.

Mother's Day and my mother's birthday were approaching and here I was behind bars, struggling to stay alive. My mother was still a patient at Monterey Care Center. With her Alzheimer's disease worsening by the day, she would not remember that I didn't visit her, but I would!

This was not like me! I had to get my act together and stop wallowing in despair. After all, I was not the only *mother* in the room. Without any doubt, however, I did hold the distinction of being the only *grandmother* in the room. I sensed that some of the young mothers were feeling depressed due to the upcoming holiday and being away from their children. So, I began to strike up conversations with some of them about their children. After hearing each sad story, we cried together. It seemed to help them and it made me realize I could pull myself together and withstand this hell hole a little while longer.

Mother's Day Behind Bars
May 9, 2010

Oh, how my heart ached to be with my mother and my daughters on Mother's Day! I thought of them every day, of course, but Mother's Day was our very special day together. During my entire life, I had never missed a Mother's Day with my mother and one or both of my daughters, Sheri and Trisha. How lucky and blessed I had always been.

There were no holidays in jail. Every day was the same – no special treatment or special food of any kind. Most of the twenty-four inmates in the dorm were mothers; they, too, were feeling the pain today. After breakfast and chores, some of the girls decided to stay up and were seated at one of the round tables with me. Since I had lived and experienced life much longer than anyone else there, I began to tell them some funny stories about my life and recite some of my favorite poems. To my surprise, the crowd grew larger as I regaled them. Their favorite poem, and mine, was William Wordsworth's excerpt from *Ode to Immortality*:

> Though nothing can bring back the hour,
> Of splendor in the grass
> Glory in the flower,
> We will grieve not...
> Rather find strength in what remains behind.

The girls' favorite funny story was about my addiction to Nicorette gum years ago. Many funny things happened to me because of that addiction. One of the inmates wrote a special poem for me. It was so sweet my tears began to flow; I guess my reservoir was not dry after all. Several more inmates wrote poems and letters to me which really lifted my spirits. I do believe that everything happens for a reason.

I thought, "Maybe, I'm here in jail, at this exact time and in this exact place for a very special purpose."

Linda Case

One Mother Goes Home
May 10 - 31, 2010

Every day in jail was always the same for me except for *Bible* Study class on Saturday mornings. The context of the classes was not really a study of the *Bible*, but more of a group discussion wherein our current life events were related to various sections and messages in the *Bible*. After filling out a written request form, three different times, I was finally approved in order to attend once a week.

The teacher was Cindy Davis, an angel here on earth. She maintained a full time job elsewhere and volunteered her time each Saturday at the jail. She reminded her students, "It's not just the life you live, but the love and light you give that matters." Every Saturday, she brought with her not only lots of love and light but also a non-judgmental, open ear to the various woes of the inmates. Cindy was a true messenger of love and light, a guardian angel to many souls, including myself.

For several weeks, Sheri and Albert had been painting and fixing up my mother's small house in Valleyview, a suburb of Columbus, Ohio, in preparation for my mother to move back home. Although liens had been filed on the property, they were hoping that the government would not exercise their liens and seize the property. There was not much furniture left in the big house in Grove City since we had been selling or giving away everything in preparation for the move to Mexico. Sheri and Albert moved what furniture was left and purchased basic necessities in order to set up housekeeping in Valleyview. Since the government had relieved me of all my assets, the large monthly mortgage payments had not been made on the Grove City property for several months. It was just a matter of time until the house would be in foreclosure. Eventually, I lost the Grove City house and my equity.

Everyone thought that I was going to be released on May 3, and would then be able to bring my mother home from the Monterey Care Center. Unfortunately, however, that was not to be. On May 19, Sheri and Albert "rescued" my mother and brought her home to Valleyview where she had lived for many years. Her cats were there to greet her and, according to Sheri, my mother was overjoyed. Sheri was trained as an STNA, State Tested Nursing Assistant, and had worked in nursing homes. Together with Albert, she felt certain that the two of them could give my mother the proper twenty-four hour care she now required.

The fact that my mother had Alzheimer's disease was actually a blessing in one instance: She had no concept of time. Her disease had progressed to the point that she was not aware of what month, day, or even year it was. It was a bittersweet grace because she had no idea I was in jail and had been gone more than three months. I feared it would have been the last straw for her; she had been through so much pain and sorrow. My mother did notice my absence, though. Frequently, she would ask Sheri about me. Sheri told her I was on a much needed vacation following income tax season. My mother readily accepted this answer since, for many years, that is exactly what I did following income tax season.

A Little Good News
June 2, 2010

A confidential, final copy of the *Presentence Investigation Report* arrived in the mail from Attorney Smith. The offense was Count 1: Willfully Making a False Statement. The *Final Sentencing Recommendation* was five months imprisonment, five months home confinement, two years of supervised release, and a special assessment of $100. There would be no probation sentence.

Finally, some **great** news! The best news I had gotten in months! A week later, another letter arrived from Attorney Smith stating that my actual sentencing hearing had been scheduled for Friday, July 9 at 9:15a.m.

"Yippee!" I yelled. "In less than a month, I'll be FREE!"

Attorney Smith's letter also reiterated what he had recently told me, "As you know, I will be out of the country at this time and Alex Newton* from my office will be handling the sentencing."

I could not believe that my attorney would not be present for my sentencing. He was going to be out of the country for an entire month. When I registered my disappointment about it, he simply said, "We can reschedule the sentencing for a future date after my return or you can be represented by my associate."

Those were my only two choices. Rescheduling meant that I would remain in jail for an additional month at minimum, depending on the judge's court calendar. I vehemently did not accept that option. So I was stuck with a brand new attorney at my sentencing.

For the first time since my arrest four months earlier, there was light at the end of the tunnel. I had a termination date, a date the hopeless feelings would end, when the daily wondering of what was going to happen next could cease. Everything terrible has a termination point.

Of course, sentencing did not necessarily mean I would be released immediately. However, one of the federal inmates with lots of prior experience and knowledge in these matters informed me, "Judges almost always go along with the *Sentencing Recommendations* and *Sentencing Guidelines* submitted by the U. S. Probation Officer and Sentencing Guidelines Specialist." I was counting on the application of this standard in my case.

One Kind Deed
June 16, 2010

Sheri picked Bobby up at the Columbus airport. A few days earlier, he had called Sheri and asked for financial help. He told her he was destitute, had recently separated from his wife, and wanted to come back to Columbus to live. Bobby's father, daughter, grandmother, two stepbrothers, their wives, and other paternal relatives lived in Columbus or nearby. According to Bobby, none of them would agree to help him anymore. Sheri sent Bobby the money for his flight to Columbus. After he arrived, she offered him my bed to sleep in, my car to drive, and paid him to help out with my mother's care.

Sheri did not know that Bobby had set me up, not once but twice, with the U.S. Marshals. She was unaware that his actions had, ultimately, led to the marshals' suspicion and subsequent investigation into my life, giving them the means to have me incarcerated. The situation was ironic, I thought, but I did not say anything to her about it. I still felt very sorry for Bobby; he had always been so dependent on Becky. And, just as I have forgiven Becky over the years, I have also forgiven Bobby.

It was ironic, too, I felt, that childhood memories of Becky's mischievous actions towards me, followed by my mother insisting that I forgive Becky, continually found their way into my thoughts through-out this entire ordeal.

Sheri never knew about my communications with Becky after my sister's disappearance. Sheri would have been horrified if she was aware of my contact with Becky. She knew, better than anyone, all the unkind things Becky had done to me over the years. Had she known I was risking my own integrity and freedom to help Becky, Sheri would have had me committed or turned me in to the marshals herself!

Barely Hanging On
June 21, 2010

The closest friend I made in jail was released from the Delaware County Jail on June 21. Like me, Lara* had never been arrested. She was sentenced to ninety days in jail for something very unusual. She and her daughter, Cindy* had accidentally come across an aged, abandoned shack which was full of beautiful, old glassware. When she saw it, Lara said she thought, "Oh, what pretty glassware! It must have been abandoned a long time ago by the looks of it." She and Cindy were loading the pretty glassware into the trunk of their car when the owner of the pretty glassware appeared out of the blue, and minutes later, so did the police.

She had thirty more days to serve when, unexpectedly, the CO announced, "Lara, pack it up!" Her attorney got her released after serving only sixty days.

For those sixty days, she had been my rock. When one of us was depressed, the other was always there to cry with, and to help survive another day, another moment. I was happy for Lara, but I was going to miss her terribly.

Soon after she was gone, I fell apart again. I began to cry and screamed, "I just can't take this place another minute!" There had been so many disappointments, from the previous four months, and now Lara was gone. I became hysterical and verbally expressed my feelings of despair and hopelessness to everyone throughout the dorm.

Thankfully for me, Officer Thompson was the CO on duty. She sat with me for a long time and saved me, once again, from isolation and the dreaded "pickle suit."

Lara was a true friend. She came to visit me every week after her discharge. In order to survive, she knew how important it was for me to have a basic connection with the outside world. I was infinitely grateful for her kindnesses.

Anticipation
June 25, 2010

Once again, a letter came from Attorney Smith along with a copy of the *United States' Sentencing Memorandum and Motion for Downward Departure and Motion for Unsealing* (14 pages) and *Sentencing Memorandum* (43 pages).

The *Sentencing Memorandum* began with:

Defendant, Linda L. Case, by and through undersigned counsel, respectfully submits this sentencing memorandum in support of a sentence below or at recommended sentence suggested by the Final Presentence Investigation Report. Such a sentence is sufficient, but not greater than necessary to comply with the purposes of 18 U.S.C. 3553(a). Additionally, it is anticipated that the United States Attorney's Office will recommend a 5K1. For the reasons that follow, the defense requests a sentence below or equal to the recommended sentence that is proposed in the Final Presentence Investigation, as such a sentence complies with the Sentencing Guidelines.

If all went well, I could be going home in just two weeks! I could not wait to hear those much anticipated words by the Corrections Officer upon my release, "Case, pack it up!" To fill my time and keep my spirits up, I began to make lists of things I wanted to do, people I wanted to hug, things I wanted to eat, and people I wanted to thank. Several of those on the list of people to thank were female Correction Officers at Delaware County Jail. Although it seemed to me that most of the COs were on some kind of power trip and not very nice, there were a few who proved to be compassionate human beings; they helped keep me alive through six months of hell. I expected to never forget Officers Ripley*, Thompson, Strader* and McCutcheon*.

Cruel and Unusual Punishment
July 9, 2010

July 12 would mark the five-month anniversary of my incarceration; that was three days after my July 9 court date for sentencing. Since the sentencing recommendations *Sentencing Recommendations* were "five months incarceration," everyone, including me, was certain I would be going home with time served. It was a long night, and I felt like a kid on Christmas Eve, too excited to sleep. I spent the night before the sentencing packing the few things I would be taking home with me, mostly pictures, cards and letters. Everything else I gave to one of the indigent inmates, including my hard-won personal t-shirts, socks and toiletries.

The morning finally arrived, and the usual procedures followed. This would be my last time in the Freezer, Hallelujah! Even though outdoor temperatures had been hovering above 100 degrees for weeks, every day in the dorm was so cold that I kept the wool blanket over my shoulders most of the day. I pictured myself as Scarlett O'Hara in the movie, *Gone with the Wind,* when she stood in the empty garden, hungry and shaking her fist; I said to myself, "When I get out of here, as long as I live, I'll never be cold like this again!"

According to my new attorney, it was helpful to have as many family members and friends at the sentencing as possible. It was supposed to influence the judge's decision in a positive way. Sheri had gone into action once again. When I walked into the courtroom, hands cuffed and legs shackled, I was flabbergasted by the number of supporters who showed up on my behalf. My daughter, Trisha and my grandson, Aaron, came all the way from Georgia. Another dear friend, Ed, a well-known and respected former businessman in Columbus, had even prepared a written statement to read to the judge on my behalf. I was inexpressibly grateful to see all the faces of those who cared so much about what happened to me! Sheri had also arranged a celebration for everyone, later that day.

My sentencing was scheduled for 9:15 a.m., rescheduled for 11:15 a.m., and rescheduled again, after lunch, for 1:00 p.m. It was no accident that mine was to be the last case of the day for the judge. Finally, my name was called to stand before the judge with Attorney Newton. I had prepared a brief, written statement for the judge which I was allowed to read. My hands were shaking as I wept and as I read my notes.

"Your Honor, I have accepted full responsibility for lying to Drew Shadwick, United States Marshall. I sincerely apologize to Drew, also to Doug Squires, Prosecuting Attorney, to you, Judge Marbley and to this Court.

"Since my arrest, I've cooperated fully with the U.S. Marshals and will continue to help them as long as it takes, until my sister is apprehended and sent to prison.

"I'm so very sorry! Once I am able to, I will do everything in my power, for the rest of my life, to make this right for everyone, especially my family. I respectfully request that you allow me the opportunity to go home, to begin healing and earning trust back, to resume my responsibilities and make amends. Thank you."

The judge cited the charge against me, read parts of the *Sentencing Memorandums* and briefly discussed the facts of the case. The judge said he "found it ironic that Case's blind loyalty to an undeserving sister has caused (Case) to serve time when that sister has yet to serve her prison term." What happened next was a totally unexpected, and unbelievable, shock to everyone!

U.S. District Judge Algenon L. Marbley imposed the following sentence:

The defendant is hereby committed to the custody of the United States Bureau of Prisons to be imprisoned for a term of six months. Supervised release: Upon release from imprisonment, the defendant shall be on supervised release for a term of three years. As a special condition of supervised release the defendant shall serve the first eight months in the home confinement program with electronic monitoring. Monetary penalty: Count One, $100.00 Assessment

Remember, the *Sentence Recommendation* was only five months imprisonment, not six. Judge Marbley also increased the home confinement sentence from five months to eight months; he added the requirement for electronic monitoring, and he increased the supervised release from two years to three years!

The moments that followed passed in a blur for me. As I was being escorted out of the courtroom, I vaguely remember seeing Sheri crying and the disappointed look on all the faces of family and friends. Our day of celebration turned into another day of suffering and extreme sorrow, not just for me but for all those who loved and cared for me, as well. Cindy, the *Bible* study teacher, was at the sentencing; she told me later, "It was all I could do to restrain myself from getting up out of my chair and saying something to that judge. He was so mean to you."

Everyone back at the jail was in shock as well. They all felt that the judge's sentence, for telling one lie, was extremely cruel and excessive punishment, especially in view of the fact that I had no prior criminal record of any kind. After five months of one disappointment after another, I was not at all sure that I would be able to pull myself through another thirty-three days in hell.

Sheri and I had spoken on the phone every single day while I was in jail, barring one or two days immediately following my arrest. I did not phone Sheri that evening or the next. There would be no hiding my deep depression from her, and I felt she needed some time to deal with her own depression and disappointment.

When we spoke again, Sheri was her usual positive, cheerful self, reminding me of all the many positive reasons for me to remain mentally and physically healthy.

"You have so many people out here who love you and want you back in their lives again." She reminded me. "Stay strong for me, Mom. I need you, Grandma needs you, Sonny Boy and the kitties need you, too. Promise me that you'll continue reading your daily meditations, your grateful list and exercising daily. And remember, no matter how bad or how good things are, they will change!"

Prison vs. Jail
July 10, 2010

July 10, 2010, *The Columbus Dispatch* wrote a headline, "Fugitive's Sister Sent to Prison for Lying, Mexico Rendezvous Planned with Former Exec, Emails Show. Parts of the article were reported as follows:

A federal government attempt to reel in fugitive Rebecca S. Parret by charging her 66-year-old sister with obstruction hasn't panned out so far.

The sister, Linda Case of Grove City, was sent to prison yesterday while Parrett remains free, probably in Mexico.

U.S. District Judge Algenon L. Marbley sentenced Case to six months in prison, followed by eight months of house arrest and three years of probation after she is released. Case will receive credit for the four months she has spent in jail. 'I accept full responsibility for lying,' she said in court. 'I'm so very sorry.'

Marbley said he found it ironic that Case's 'blind loyalty to an undeserving sister has caused (Case) to serve time when that sister has yet to serve her prison term.' John E. Smith, Case's attorney, argued in court documents that Parrett took advantage of her sister's kind-heartedness.

'Ms Parrett has a history of manipulating people and situations for her own benefit,' Smith wrote in a sentencing memorandum for Case. 'During the days when Ms. Parrett was making an outrageous amount of money as a result of her company, Ms. Parrett simply ignored her family and treated them like 'West Virginia hillbillies.'

Case began emailing Parrett after her disappearance to reassure their mother that Parrett was alive, the memorandum says.

Since I had already served five months of my six-month prison sentence at the Delaware County Jail, there was not enough time for the Bureau of Prisons to complete a transfer. So, the entire six-month sentence was fulfilled at Delaware County Jail. According to some fellow inmates who had been in both prison and jail, prison was a much better place to serve out your sentence, by far.

Each day seemed like a week. Each morning, another day was anxiously crossed off on the calendar I had made for myself. Sheri and I became terribly frustrated when none of the authorities, not the U.S. Marshals, Judge Marbley, or the Delaware County Jail Officers could tell us the exact date and time of my release. Finally, after many phone calls and emails between Sheri and the Bureau of Prisons, Sheri was told my release date would be Saturday, August 14, 2010 at 9:00 a.m.

My term in jail would amount to **182 days, six months, two days, one hour, and five minutes!** All of it as punishment for telling a lie.

Free at Last!
August 14, 2010

U nable to sleep all night the night before I was to be released, I lay in my bunk, eyes closed. Projected onto my eyelids, I viewed what seemed to be a video recording of the previous six months of my life. I had reached the depths of despair and lived through it! The anticipation of the day ahead was overwhelming.

At 4:30 a.m., I could restrain myself no longer and arose from my bunk for the very last time. Officer McCutcheon was on duty in the dorm so we talked, very quietly, until the lights came on and everyone else got up for breakfast. After chores were completed, many of the girls stayed with me instead of going back to bed as they usually did. We hugged, cried and promised to keep in touch.

Finally, around 8:30 a.m., Officer McCutcheon spoke those magic words, "Case, pack it up!" Then, to my surprise, everyone in the dorm started clapping and cheering. The door opened, and Officer Ripley appeared, smiling from ear to ear. She was to walk me to the front office for final release papers, a change of clothing, then down several halls and out the front door of the jail. Officer Ripley had deliberately scheduled to work that Saturday morning just so she could be my escort. I was extremely grateful to Ms. Ripley for many things, including this final kindness.

My first view of the outside world in more than six months was Sheri, Albert and Sonny Boy waiting beside their car, in the parking lot just outside the front door. When Sonny Boy saw me, he got so excited that he ran toward me, jumped up and knocked me down to the concrete sidewalk. One of my shoes went flying through the air. Together, we all began laughing and crying at the same time. It was quite an emotional moment. For six long months, I had been denied the basic need for connection with my loved ones. We hugged, laughed and cried for a long time before heading for home.

Freedom is the ability to wake up every day and *decide* what to do with the day. When I lost my freedom, there were no words to describe the feelings of hopelessness and helplessness that permeated every moment of every day behind bars. I am forever grateful for my freedom, for the ability to breathe fresh air, the love and kindness of many family and friends, my health, my strength to survive adversity, the opportunity to move forward and make something good out of bad rubbish, and for the thirty-nine other things listed in my daily *Grateful Prayer*.

Because of my actions, my house is in foreclosure, my equity is gone, and my retirement funds and savings have been entirely consumed by attorney fees. I paid a very high price for my bad choices but blame no one but myself. Another important daily prayer in my life now is the *Serenity Prayer* – "to give me the strength to accept the things I cannot change, the courage to change the things I can, and the wisdom to know the difference."

Today, and every day, is a treasure. It was a new day, a beautiful, warm and sunny August day. On the drive home from the jail, we stopped only once for a large cup of regular coffee for me, the first I had in six months. Most of the day was spent at home on the back porch, sitting in my rocking chair, breathing, as the fresh, free air washed over me. This was my "happy place" where I was surrounded by potted flowers with a close-up view of birds and squirrels going about their day. Later in the afternoon, a light, soft, summer rain appeared as if on cue. I had been waiting for this moment for a long time and actually began to dance in the rain. My storm had passed.

My dreams of living in sunny Mexico are gone with the wind. They remain behind, but I will grieve not. Home is not a place; rather, it is where your heart lives. America is my home. My heart lives here surrounded by family and friends. There is truly no place like home! As author Anna Sewell wrote in *Black Beauty*, "I have nothing to fear and here my story ends. My troubles are all over and I am at home."

About the Author

Linda L. Case is the former President/Owner of Case Accounting and Tax Service. She was featured in "A Salute to Women in Business" published by *The Columbus Dispatch* newspaper. She is a graduate of Ohio State University and life member of the Ohio State Alumni Association. While attending Ohio State, Linda was featured in the school newspaper, promoting the benefits of education. She is a member of the Atlanta Writers Club and continues to promote her career as a writer by participating in creative writing programs. She is a past treasurer for the Public Accountants Society of Ohio, a past member of the International Toastmistress Club and has experience presenting seminars and workshops. Linda is represented by Loiacono Literary Agency.

Epilogue

In 1950, the FBI began to post their "Most Wanted Fugitives" list. There are 494 names on that list. Only eight are women.

October 26, 2010 - Rebecca (Becky) Parrett was arrested by Mexican immigration officials in Ajijic, Jalisco, Mexico.

December 23, 2010 – "Rebecca Parrett appeared, in person, before Judge Algenon L. Marbley in U.S. District Court for a face-to-face reading of her 25-year prison sentence. Marbley saved his sharpest criticism of Parrett for her treatment of her sister, Linda Case.

'The worst thing,' the Judge said, 'is the way you used and manipulated your sister.'
'If you want to apologize to anyone, you should apologize to your sister,' Marbley told Parrett." December 24th edition of *The Columbus Dispatch*

January, 6, 2011 - Gary Green (Rebecca's husband) was arrested in California and charged with lying to government investigators about his contact with his wife while she was hiding in Mexico. He is accused of supplying her with clothing and large amounts of cash.

February 17, 2011 - Rebecca Parrett was sent to Federal prison in Dublin, California, to begin serving her 25-year sentence.

April 15, 2011 - Linda Case was released from house arrest after serving eight months with electronic monitoring. She remained on probation until August 14, 2013.

April 30, 2012 - Gary Green was sentenced to only four months house arrest by a federal judge in California.

May 17, 2012 - Linda L. Case's Motion to Terminate Supervision (probation) was filed.

August 20, 2012 - Motion to Terminate Supervision (probation) granted by Judge Marbley.

Appendix

1. Hand-delivered Lien, October 2006
2. 2. Letter from Mom: Possible Eviction From Her House, November 2006
3. *Columbus Dispatch* Article: Becky's Disappearance, May 2008
4. Becky featured on America's Most Wanted, May 2008
5. Letter from Becky: Instructions to Me, July 2008
6. Letter to Retain Attorney, September 2008
7. E-mails from Sheri re: Trip to Mexico, May & June 2009
8. Letter from ABC News Producer, May 2009
9. Articles in Local Newspapers re: My Arrest, February 2010
10. Sealed Document, February 2010
11. My Letter to Judge Marbley, March 2010
12. Sheri's letter to Family & Judge Marbley, April 2010
13. Shelly's Poem, Mother's Day, May 2010
14. Articles in Local Newspapers re: Sentencing, July 2010

Item 1.1

U.S. Department of Justice

United States Attorney
Southern District of Ohio

303 Marconi Boulevard	*(614) 469-5715*
Suite 200	*FAX (614) 469-5240*
Columbus, Ohio 43215	

October 31, 2006

Nellie M. Lamon
████████████████
Columbus, Ohio 43204

Re: United S████████████████████ Poulsen, et al.
    Rebecca Parrett / Criminal Action No. CR-2-06-129
    In re. 2813 Elliott Avenue, Columbus, Ohio 43204

TO THE PARTY ADDRESSED:

Enclosed please find a file-stamped copy of the Plaintiff
United States of America's Notice of Lis Pendens with regard to the
property located at 2813 Elliott Avenue, Columbus, Ohio.

Should you have any questions and/or comments please contact
me at the phone number indicated above.

Very truly yours,

GREGORY G. LOCKHART
United States Attorney

Dale E. Williams, Jr.
Assistant United States Attorney

Enclosure

Item 1.2

IN THE COURT OF COMMON PLEAS
FRANKLIN COUNTY, OHIO

IN RE: REBECCA S. PARRETT 06LPC-9-00006

NOTICE OF LIS PENDENS

Know all men that the United States of America, Plaintiff in the hereinafter styled cause, does hereby give notice of Lis Pendens, by the Notice filed in the Clerk's Office of the Court of Common Pleas of Franklin County, Ohio, by virtue of a certain cause, in the United States District Court for the Southern District of Ohio, Eastern Division, being Criminal Action No. CR-2-06-129, the title of which is <u>United States of America v. Lance K. Poulsen, et al.</u>, one of the general objects thereof to forfeit to the United States of America, ████████████ Columbus, Ohio 43204, pursuant to the provisions of 18 U.S.C. §981, §982 and 28 U.S.C. §2461. See Attachment A, a certified copy of the Indictment, CR-2-06-129.

The name of the person whose estate is intended ~~to be affected~~ ████████ is Rebecca S. Parrett.

The real property to be forfeited and to which this NOTICE is directed is described as follows:

Real Property and improvements thereon known and numbered as ████████████ Columbus, Ohio 43204, and legally described as:

SITUATED IN THE IN THE STATE OF OHIO, COUNTY OF FRANKLIN AND IN THE TOWNSHIP OF FRANKLIN, WHICH IS DESCRIBED AS:

1

Item 1.3

BEING LOT NUMBER THREE (3), OF THE AMENDED LOTS TWENTY-SIX (26), TWENTY-SEVEN (27), AND TWENTY-EIGHT (28) OF OAK KNOLL ADDITION, AS THE SAME IS NUMBERED AND DELINEATED UPON THE RECORDED PLAT THEREOF, OF RECORD IN PLAT BOOK 17, PAGE 379, RECORDER'S OFFICE, FRANKLIN COUNTY, OHIO.

Parcel # 144-042, known as ▓▓▓▓▓▓▓▓▓▓ Avenue, Columbus, Ohio 43204

Prior Instrument Reference: Book 281, Page 2262 of the Official Records of Delaware County, Ohio

Dated this _15th_ day of _September_, 2006.

Respectfully submitted,

GREGORY G. LOCKHART
United States Attorney

DALE E. WILLIAMS, JR. (0020094)
Assistant United States Attorney
Attorney for Plaintiff
303 Marconi Boulevard, Suite 200
Suite 200
Columbus, Ohio 43215
(614) 469-5715

STATE OF OHIO   )
) SS.
COUNTY OF FRANKLIN)

On this _15_ day of _September_, 2006, Dale E. Williams, Jr., Assistant United States Attorney, who, being first duly sworn, signed the above NOTICE OF LIS PENDENS and acknowledged the same before me, a Notary Public, in my presence.

Notary Public

DEBORAH F. SANDERS, Attorney-at-law
NOTARY PUBLIC — STATE OF OHIO
My Commission has no expiration date
Section 147.03 R. C.

2

Item 2

Linda:

I know that you have
this phone number & I wondered
if you could call & ask her
one thing for me.

Can someone evict me from
this? And if so how long do
I have? It is worrying me to
death. I can't hardly sleep & I
am a nervous wreck

She told me one time that I
could live here as long as I
lived. It would be wonderful if
that were true.

Please do this for me before I
crack up.

Please, please, please.   Love,
                                 Mom

Item 3.1

Where is showy fugitive? Her past yields few clues

Sunday, May 18, 2008 3:25 AM

CAREFREE, Ariz. -- The day after being convicted in Columbus of the nation's largest fraud of a privately held company, Rebecca S. Parrett boarded a plane headed for this Phoenix suburb.

Carefree has a name befitting the life Parrett seemingly tried to create.

She bought a $3 million home perched on a mountain ridge and built it into a $6 million estate. The main quarters, guest house and stable are a mix of the Southwest and the expensive elegance of the corporate world she never completely left behind.

The manor became a centerpiece for Parrett's passions: hosting gatherings of artists, holding upscale fundraisers for animal-rescue groups, and occasionally housing missionaries from the evangelical church she supported.

Her trip to Carefree in mid-March, however, was supposed to be an excursion. Federal Judge Algenon L. Marbley had allowed her to return to her Arizona home only while she was waiting to be sentenced.

Parrett arrived. But she didn't stay long.

Vanishing act

She landed at the Phoenix airport in the early-morning hours of Saturday, March 15 -- less than 48 hours after a jury found her guilty of securities fraud linked to the collapse of the health-care financing company National Century Financial Enterprises.

A day later, she disappeared.

Federal officials think that Parrett, 59, flew the coop to avoid a sentence that could be as much as 75 years -- effectively a life

The fugitive

- *Who she is:* Rebecca S. Parrett, 59, was one of the founders and a former director of National Century Financial Enterprises, which collapsed in 2002. She previously had worked for Grant Hospital.
- *What happened:* The company offered financing to small hospitals, clinics and nursing homes by buying their accounts receivable and giving them cash to cover expenses. National Century

Item 4

Item 5.1

Linda,

I'm so happy we've been close these last few months. It really has meant a lot to me and I want to thank you for allowing me to stay in your home.

It's Saturday, March 15th. By the time you read this, assuming you ever get it, I will be gone. I just got home late last night from Ohio and my grief and depression are off the charts. Gary has tried to do everything possible to help me and he's suffering deeply as well. I want to try to make today and tonight as good as possible because I may never see him again.

I think he'll be ok because he has his girls and I know he'll care for the animals as best he can.

I could be wrong again. Heaven knows, I've made many bad decisions since this whole process started, but I am planning to leave tomorrow morning and start driving .... To where, I don't know ...... hopefully an isolated, remote area that I can just pray and try to regain my mental and physical health.

There are a lot of areas in northern and southern Arizona that are still pretty remote. Maybe I'll find something. I just can't take this any more. I've been coughing up blood in the mornings and have had several episodes of severe chest pain. I know if I don't get away from this soon, it's going to kill me.

I never thought I'd ever think of suicide, but even that's crossed my mind a number of times. The pain is just so horrible, I can't stand it. They might as well have taken a knife and stabbed me with it because even though you're alive on the outside, you're dead on the inside.

I don't want to cause you any more pain. Heaven knows I've caused enough pain and humiliation for the entire family to last a lifetime. If my disc makes its way back to you, I hope you'll help me once more.

I had been working on a manuscript of what was happening since almost the beginning. Everything bad that could happen 'did' happen, but I can only go forward and not backwards, although I wish more than anything I could have done some things differently.

I've written a letter to ██████ Mom and Bob that I'd like for you to give them. I'd also like for you to send Gary a copy of the manuscript. He should know what really happened as well. I tried to shield him from the horror of it all and didn't talk very much about it at home, but I want him to know the truth. He knows I'm innocent, but I think it will help him understand much better after he reads it.

Item 5.2

████ has been a great friend over the years and I miss our good times together. Her relationship with ████████ might open a door to get help. I don't know, but it might be worth a try. If you let her see a printed copy of the manuscript, she could take it to ████ and ask him if there's anything he could do. I know he's a powerful man in Washington and maybe he can somehow help me.

If not, maybe the Democrats would be interested in it. I previously met Bill Clinton on two occasions. Or maybe if the democrats get elected, there could be some opportunity for someone to help. I just don't know. People don't seem to care anymore if they destroy a person's life.

My letter to Bob will hopefully help him in some way deal with all of this. I love him deeply but I know I was not a great mother for him, even though I did the best I could. Unless he stops drinking, he will always have problems with relationships and dealing with daily reality. I've tried to help him and be there for him his whole life, but now I can't be there any more. I will pray for him every day and hope to God that he stays safe and well.

Hopefully my letter to mom will help her deal with the situation better. I know her memory is getting very bad and I'm very sorry that I'm adding to her health issues, but there's just nothing I can do any more. I know she doesn't want me to go to jail for something I did not do.

I know once I start down the road, there's no turning back. I'm very afraid, but I'm even more afraid of going to prison with my health as it is and putting mom through another ordeal like Dannie's. I think it's less pain for her if she doesn't know what happens to me versus watching me die one day at a time in prison or a prison hospital.

████████ is an attorney in the ████████ area. We went to high school together and had remained friends over the years. If you need help with mom or other matters, he would be a good person for you to use.

You could probably share the manuscript with ████ if you ████████ e of you can reserve a website domain name for Victim of Justice. In the event something good might happen with the manuscript, it would be nice to help others who have been victims as well.

Reverend Darryl Delhousaye is President of the Phoenix Seminary. I told him I was working on a book and asked him if he would be willing to write something inspirational for it and he said he would. After you talk with ████ about the manuscript, you might contact Darryl and ask him to write a few pages.

Also, if you wanted to write something from the family perspective, that might be a good idea as well. Maybe, maybe not.

Item 5.3

I don't know a lot about publishing, but Pastor Darryl and ██████ are both experienced in that field and could probably help. I know you need to get an isbn number to properly identify it. There's a website for booksurge.com that's owned by Amazon. It's a self publishing business that might also be an option.

I really want our family, friends and anyone who's ever known me to have an opportunity to read the book and know the real truth as it relates to me. Please make sure that happens somehow. It's very important to me to know that they know the truth and no matter what happens, please do that for me. And, of course, make sure both of the grandchildren get a copy to read.

When you're dealing with something like this, you feel backed into a corner with no place to go. I can understand why people resort to suicide sometimes. When you feel your life is over and all you're doing is causing pain for the people you love, you can only take it for so long before you're broken down totally.

There's no way to communicate, but I will check the internet for Columbus Dispatch classified personals on the first and third Friday of each month. It's the only thing I can think of at the moment that might be a way for you to let me know if Bob Bennett can help. Don't try to put personal information there because it would be too hard for both of us. If you happen to put something there and I don't reply somehow, hopefully it'll be because I just haven't figured out a way to do it and not because I was not able to see it.

I will also make sure I keep your phone numbers on my possession somehow or give it to someone I might meet along the way. In the event something happens to me, hopefully someone will contact you or Gary.

I love you all so much and wish I had my life back again so we could all grow old together. Forgive me for causing you all so much suffering. I am truly sorry.

I hope you get this letter and will give the letters to the various people and try to get the manuscript printed and distributed. I know it's a lot to ask, but the only thing that matters to me now is to make sure people that I care about will know the true story.

Take care of yourself. I'll pray for you every day. God Bless.

Item 6.1

August 20, 2008

Dear ▪▪▪ ▪▪▪

I am Becky Parrott's sister. I believe
I met you once, a very long time ago.

I'm sure you're familiar with her
trial, subsequent conviction and the fact
that she has been missing since March.

On July 27, 2008, her husband, Gary,
brought two of Becky's elderly cats to me
to care for. He also brought approximately
25 large boxes of her "personal" stuff
from Arizona. It took me several
weeks to unpack the boxes. Inside
one of the boxes, in an envelope with
my name on it, was a CD. Contained
on the CD was a manuscript, titled
"Victim of Justice", and letters to me,
Mom, Bob (her son) and ▪▪▪ (her best
friend). In the letter to me, she said,
if I ever needed an attorney, to contact
you... that you two had been friends
since high school.

Before I do anything with the

Item 6.2

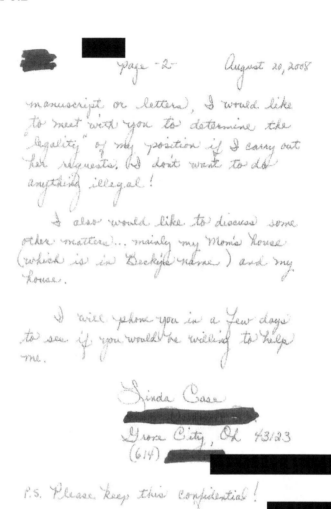

page -2-   August 20, 2008

manuscript or letters), I would like
to meet with you to determine the
"legality" of my position if I carry out
her requests, (I don't want to do
anything illegal!

I also would like to discuss some
other matters)... mainly my Mom's house
(which is in Becky's name) and my
house.

I will phone you in a few days
to see if you would be willing to help
me.

Linda Case

Grove City, OH 43123
(614)

P.S. Please keep this confidential!

Item 7.1

> **Subject:** RE: House Sale
> **From:** Kent, Sheri ███████████████
> To: linda_loophole@yahoo.com;
> **Date:** Wednesday, May 6, 2009 3:53 PM

Hi Mom,

I didn't get your e-mail until today... I was home sick with my cold yesterday. I started to feel better by the afternoon and then our first fire of 2009 broke out and there was a lot of smoke. I closed the windows and turned on the air purifier you got us - it was awesome! The temperature outside also went UP in the evening instead of down. It was mid 70s during the day and by 7:30 at night it was **88** degrees. So we were all sweating our asses off inside with no air conditioning and no fresh air. The air purifier saved us all. I can't believe we are already dealing with fires out here and it is just May. That's pretty early in the year to be dealing with fires. We are all okay and it's not too close - where we live is not even in an evacuation warning area - but where I work is — and yet, I am at work today. These MF-ers don't want to pay us to stay at home and be safe so here we are! I will keep you posted if things change. No need to worry.

I am very glad to hear you are motivated about the house. Selling it will sure set a lot more things in motion for us all instead of being in limbo. So is the $25k your cut or our cut? I looked online a week or so ago and I think the balance owed was $221 k. What are you thinking of setting as the asking price? I would really hate to lose my investment in it. Let's make sure the outcome is one we are both happy with! We really have to use The Secret to bring the right buyer at the right price -soon. We are a little low on funds right now. Albert hasn't been paid in 2 weeks at his job and with Marley being sick and all of our other extras our savings has been going in the wrong direction for the last month. But if there is an expense that you need to take on to sell the house and you need some money from me - let me know. I 'll do what I can to help out. I heard from the IRS Monday -1 missed that woman's call again (I swear -they must have cameras in my office because she called as soon as I stepped away from my desk!) but she left me a voicemail that said I should have it (my check) in two weeks ... that is Monday May 18th! Keep thinking positive thoughts on that one for me too.

Since I was home yesterday (sick day) I finished re-reading The Secret. I am trying really hard to be positive and visualize, etc. What makes it hard is this JOB. I really don't like being here. It isn't like other jobs I have had in the past - this place is like one long continuous negative Twilight Zone episode. I have already written my letter of resignation -1 just need a few things to fall into place (sell house, IRS check) and then we can close this chapter and move on to the next chapter in our lives. I really would like to come back to Ohio if I get enough $$.and help you get your stuff together and help with grandma and just take~a freakin* caravan down to Mexico. ^Maybe you and I could take a re-con trip ahead of time and leave Albert back to take care of Grandma, the cats' and dog? It's hard to settle on a place when you haven't been there. I do have a feeling that everything is going to work out for us and in a year or so from now when we are looking back at this mess we had to get through to get there I think we will really appreciate what we have even more.

Well, I know you are probably playing bridge Friday - but tell the caregiver to keep an eye out for a package coming your way. Just a little sumptin, sumptin for my mommy and grandma. I really wish I could be there with you to celebrate Mother's Day Sunday and grandma's birthday next week. I had every intention of being there but - my coworker is getting married and leaving the country for a month. Oh well, we will celebrate for the rest of our lives really soon!

Have a great day Sunday - I will be thinking of you. I love you very much mom! I miss you too much really. I am very grateful that you are one of my best friends and I miss playing with you!

:)

Your Daughter, Sheri

Item 7.2

From: Kent, Sheri ███████████████
Subject: Some Beach...
To: "Linda Case"
<linda_loophole@yahoo.com>
Date: Friday, May 22,2009,6:40 PM

Hey Mom,
I was just looking through this website and got really excited to get the hey outta here! Go to www.hotetsantafeinfo.com/puertoescondido and check out the cool info and photos. This hotel has *a* mostly vegetarian/seafood restaurant even! They also have a webcam that looks out from one of their decks that I check out every day I am at work for live shots of that beach. I really think this might be it... our "some beach" somewhere!

Albert had *a* really good Idea the other day ... he said I should take a trip down and check things out. I have some vacation coming In August -I could fly down solo and take lots of pictures and video and just explore all over the area - find out the actual cost of things, talk with the locals, etc. This town has a Best Western so I think it's pretty Americanized, or at least enough for us. I actually think that's a great idea.

What are you doing this holiday weekend? Albert and I are going to LA for a BBQ at Steve and Laura's tomorrow. We are also going to "pop in" on Tyler and Travis and see how they are doing too. Sunday is our Saturday - house cleaning, laundry, chores, etc. Then Monday we are going to a garden party back up at Sunburst - Michelle needs some help gardening and weeding, so first we garden - then we party. It should be a nice weekend. I was just thinking about Memorial Days past - seems like we always got together for some sort of a cookout or something? Well, whatever you do just know I will be thinking of you. I really miss you A LOT and look forward to when we can CELEBRATE everything together!

I love you

Item 7.3

From: SK █████████████████

Subject: Fw: Yahoo! Travel Confirmation for Sheri's Trip to Ohio!

To: "Linda Case" <linda loophole@yahoo com>

Date: Wednesday, June 10,2009,11:51 AM

Hey Mom,

The other thing I wanted to tell you this morning was that I made my reservations yesterday. I will be in Ohio Thursday 8/27 and staying a week until Friday 9/4. I wanted to come home that day so I could have the 3 day weekend with Albert and the kitties before going back to work. Also, I will miss Albert's birthday on the 2nd so I didn't want to be gone too much longer after that Gotta celebrate!

Anywho, mark your calendar. This trip should be better than last time since i won't be moving Grandma anywhere and hopefully you won't be as stressed out. Maybe by then the house will be sold? Oh well, even if I spend the entire time helping you move at least I will get to see you and visit for awhile. And we have to make time for some good Italian food, and a movie at the very least.

The place I worked when I was a nurse's aid was called Emerald Crossing. It really was a nice place and they had activities and such for the residents with Alzheimer's and dementia. .Maybe you could leave grandma in the care facility until we move to Mexico? Her Social Security is plenty enough to hire a nurse to come in and take care of her. Albert sajd he would do it. It's probably better for your sanity and your health and to expedite all the things you need to take care of to let her stay there until then. She's in good

hands. It's never easy but she is at least eating and taking her medicine, right? Did she get her semi-private room yet?

Talk to you manana. That's tomorrow in Spanish. You better start learning some!

Love you,

Sheri

Item 8

May 22, 2009

Ms. Linda Case
~~[redacted]~~
Grove City, OH 43123

Ms. Nellie M Lamon
~~[redacted]~~
Columbus, OH 43204

Dear Ms. Case and Ms. Lamon:

The ABC News program "20/20" is producing a report on the search for your sister and daughter Ms. Rebecca Parrett. I am writing because I am coming to Ohio next week to meet informally with many of the people involved in the case and I am hoping you will find time to chat with me.

I don't pretend to know what this ordeal has been like for either of you, nor do I know what opinion you hold of Becky these days. But I'm hoping you'll be able to give me an unbiased understanding of who she is, where she came from, and what people should know about her. I am kind of fumbling in the dark at the moment and I need your help.

I'd like the opportunity to take you to dinner or coffee and have an off-the-record conversation, with no cameras involved. I'd like to explain how we plan to move forward with our report and answer any questions you might have.

Please give me a call at your earliest convenience at [redacted] or on my cell phone at [redacted]. I will be in the Columbus area on Tuesday and Wednesday. I look forward to chatting with you.

Sincerely,

[signature]

~~[redacted]~~
Producer
ABC News Magazines

147 Columbus Avenue New York, NY 10023-6298 (212) 456-7777 Fax (212) 456-7644

Item 9.1

Business Week
Home Top News
Bloomberg
Sister of National Century Fugitive Parrett Arrested (Update2)
February 12, 2010, 04:54 PM EST
(Adds court appearance in fifth paragraph.)
By David Voreacos

Feb. 12 (Bloomberg) - U.S. authorities filed obstruction of justice and false statements charges against the sister of former National Century Financial Enterprises Inc. executive Rebecca Parrett, a fugitive sentenced to 25 years in prison.

Linda Case, 66, was arrested today at her home in Grove City, Ohio, according to a statement by Cathy Jones, acting U.S. Marshal for the Southern District of Ohio. Parrett was convicted in 2008 of defrauding investors of more than $1.9 billion, and fled after her conviction in federal court in Columbus, Ohio.

Authorities believe that Parrett, 61, who was sentenced in absentia last March 27, has been staying around Guadalajara, Mexico, according to a criminal complaint.

The sisters used coded e-mails to stay in regular contact since September 2008, according to the complaint filed in Columbus. "When interviewed by law enforcement on multiple occasions, Case denied any contact with her fugitive sister Parrett, Case denied knowing Parrett's location or condition and Case provided false and misleading information to law enforcement," according to the complaint.

Case appeared today in federal court in Columbus, where prosecutors argued she posed a risk of flight and a danger to the community, according to Assistant U.S. Attorney Douglas Squires. U.S. Magistrate Judge Terrence Kemp ordered Case jailed until a bail hearing on Feb. 16.

Authorities conducted surveillance, debriefed defendants and informants, monitored phone calls and intercepted e-mails, according to the complaint. In emails, Case discussed her financial problems and her inability to pay her mortgage.

Recreational Vehicle

Case bought a recreational vehicle and said she wanted to move to Mexico with her mother and Parrett's pets, including her cat Sammy. She sought the help of her daughter Sheri, who is married to Alberto Contreras.

"My credit is no good anymore," Case wrote on Sept. 20. "I have very little income and lots of debts."

On Jan. 11, Parrett wrote to Case: "How is Sammy? I hope he is doing OK. How about mom? Is she planning on coming with you?"

A week later, Case wrote that that "Valentine's Day is our goal" for moving to Mexico, according to the complaint. She said she would cross the border at McAllen, Texas, and drive down the east coast of Mexico to Vera Cruz.

'7 Cats and a Dog'

"We have this all worked out," Case wrote. "There's no way that Mom could make this trip with me in the RV. It's not going to be easy with 7 cats and a dog in the RV with me. As soon *as* I get settled down here, wherever that may be, and rent an apartment, I plan to fly back up here and take Mom back down with me. That's the plan."

Parrett sought to limit information to her son, Robert, and her sixth husband, Gary Green, whom she left behind in Carefree, Arizona, according to the complaint by Supervising Deputy U.S. Marshal Andrew Shadwick.

Shadwick interviewed Robert Parrett several times, and he agreed to let authorities record a call he made to Case in February 2009. Case said "nobody's heard from her," Shadwick wrote in the complaint.

On Feb. 6, Robert Parrett contacted Shadwick to say he had spoken with Case a day earlier over dinner. Case said "your Mom is OK," according to Shadwick's account in court papers.

"Robert replied, 'you know Mom's OK?'" Shadwick wrote.

'Follow Her to Mexico'

Case said she was, "then admitted, 'I will be seeing your mother again,' and Case further said that Robert would be seeing his mother again as well. Case also advised Robert that she felt the government would follow her to Mexico," Shadwick wrote.

Shadwick said today in an interview that he didn't know Parrett's exact whereabouts. "If I knew where Becky was, she'd already be in custody," Shadwick said. "I feel like we've already gotten a lot of information about her activities, her communications and what's going on in her life. I feel like it's just a matter of time before she's in custody."

National Century loaned money to struggling health-care providers and claimed to secure loans with payments that backed bonds sold to investors. Many receivables were worthless, forcing the company to use new money to pay investors. Ten executives were convicted at trial or pleaded guilty.

National Century's collapse in 2002 hastened the bankruptcies of 275 hospitals, clinics and other health-care providers, authorities say. Victims included Pacific Investment Management Co., the world's largest bond fund. Pimco lost $283 million and Credit Suisse Group AG lost $257 million, prosecutors said.

Item 9.2

The Columbus Dispatch

NATIONAL CENTURY

Sister was e-mailing fugitive, feds say

Women allegedly planned to meet soon in Mexico

Saturday, February 13, 2010 3:09 AM

BY KATHY LYNN GRAY

THE COLUMBUS DISPATCH

The sister of the fugitive National Century founder had planned to move to Mexico to be with her by Valentine's Day, officials said.

But yesterday, Linda Case, 66, of Grove City, was arrested at her home and jailed pending a detention hearing on Tuesday in federal court.

Case, who was charged with obstruction of justice and lying to investigators, was accused of e-mailing her sister Rebecca S. Parrett regularly since 2008.

Federal agents intercepted the e-mails, which indicated that Parrett was hiding in Mexico.

Assistant U.S. Attorney Douglas W. Squires, one of the prosecutors who handled the National Century trials, said yesterday that he couldn't discuss Case's arrest.

Rebecca S. Parrett was sentenced to 26 years in prison.

Criminal complaint

・ Read the complaint against Linda Case.(PDF).

Parrett, 61, has been a fugitive since disappearing after her trial in March 2008. She was convicted of crimes connected to the $1.9 billion fraud involving National Century Financial Enterprises, a company that provided financing to small health-care providers.

She was sentenced last year in absentia to 25 years in prison for nine fraud-related convictions.

National Century collapsed in November 2002, and at least 275 health-care companies failed as a result. It was the largest case of private-sector fraud in U.S. history, and 10 people were convicted because of it.

According to the criminal complaint against Case, she has been communicating with Parrett in Mexico since at least September 2008 but repeatedly has denied to law enforcement that she had any contact with Parrett or knew her location.

Sister was e-mailing fugitive, feds say | The Columbus Dispatch Page 2 of 2

As recently as Jan. 25, Case told federal agents that her sister might be living in Nicaragua or Costa Rica. In the same interview, Case said she was planning to move to Veracruz, Mexico, with her daughter and son-in-law.

The complaint says deputy U.S. marshals read e-mails between Case and Parrett, who they said used code words and phrases to disguise details. In the e-mails, Parrett told Case how to conceal their email communications and said she had moved several times because she feared being recognized.

Case and Parrett had planned to meet in Mexico, the e-mails indicated, and Parrett wanted her mother to move there also.

In the back-and-forth between the sisters in September, Parrett advised Case to get a second mortgage on her Grove City home to finance the move to Mexico.

"Just don't let people know where you are going and what you are doing," Parrett wrote.

Later that month, Parrett suggested that Case try to bring travel documents for Parrett to use, the complaint says.

"I've gotten by all this time without ever using an ID, amazing," Parrett wrote. "The thing I cannot do is travel and there is a particular place I would really like to go further south but I will explain more later."

On Jan. 18, Case wrote to Parrett that she would travel soon to Mexico with her seven cats and a dog and cross the border at McAllen, Texas. Once she was settled, she planned to fly back to the United States and "take Mom back down with me," according to the complaint. kgray@dispatch.com

Item 9.3

The Columbus Dispatch

Sister of National Century fugitive to stay in jail for now

Wednesday, February 17, 2010 3:10 AM

BY JOHN FUTTY

THE COLUMBUS DISPATCH

A Grove City woman accused of lying to investigators about her fugitive sister remained in jail yesterday after waiving a federal-court hearing to challenge her detention.

The attorney for Linda Case said he needed more time to prepare arguments to support her release from custody while awaiting trial. Joseph E. Scott said he will ask for the hearing to be rescheduled soon.

Linda Case is accused of lying to investigators.

Case, 66, is the sister of Rebecca Parrett. The National Century founder fled the country after a federal jury in March 2008 convicted her of wire and securities fraud and other crimes related to the collapse of the health-care financing company.

Federal agents arrested Case on Friday and charged her with obstruction of justice and making false statements to law enforcement after investigators intercepted e-mail communications between her and Parrett. The e-mails showed that Case, who told investigators that she didn't know where they could find her sister, was planning to meet Parrett in Mexico.

Parrett, 61, was sentenced last year in absentia to 25 years in prison.

Each charge filed against Case is punishable by up to five years in prison.

jfutty@dispatch.com

Recommend

http://www.dispatch.com/live/content/local_news/stories/2010/02/17/case.ART_ART_02-...   12/1/2010

Item 10

IN THE UNITED STATES DISTRICT COURT
FOR THE SOUTHERN DISTRICT OF OHIO
EASTERN DIVISION

JAMES BONINI
CLERK

2010 FEB 25 P 12 06

UNITED STATES OF AMERICA	:	No: 2:10-cr [illegible] U.S. DIST. COURT EAST DIV. COLUMBUS
Plaintiff,	:	
	:	JUDGE MARBLEY
vs.	:	
	:	
LINDA L. CASE	:	18 U.S.C. § 1001
Defendant.	:	False Statements

INFORMATION

THE UNITED STATES ATTORNEY CHARGES:

COUNT 1
False Statements

Beginning on or about March 9, 2009, through and including January 25, 2010, in the Southern District of Ohio, in a matter within the jurisdiction of the United States Department of Justice and the United States Marshals Service, Defendant LINDA L. CASE did knowingly and willfully make a false, fraudulent and fictitious material statement and representation to federal investigators investigating the whereabouts of fugitive Rebecca L. Parrett, by denying knowing that Parrett was residing in the country of Mexico, when in fact LINDA L. CASE knew Parrett was avoiding custody and avoiding service of a twenty-five (25) year term of imprisonment by residing in Mexico.

All in violation of Title 18, United States Code, Section 1001(a)(2) and Section 2.

CARTER M. STEWART
United States Attorney

GARY L. SPARTIS
Columbus Branch Chief

Item 11.1

Re: Linda Case.

COPY

March 19, 2010

Dear Judge Marbley,

Thank you for taking your valuable time to read the "real" story behind my actions regarding my sister, Rebecca Parrett.

In 2002, I was living in Buford, Georgia, near my two daughters and grandchildren.

On November 10, 2002, my brother, Dan, died of leukemia at OSU James Cancer Clinic. Five days later, my sister's company, National Century Financial Enterprises, was raided and closed down. At this point, my mother's health began to decline rapidly.

Before my mother died, I had not spoken one word to Becky for four years. Over the past twenty some years, we rarely saw or spoke to each other. We lived in separate worlds the majority of our adult lives.

In May 2004, I returned to Columbus for mom's 80th birthday. She had lost a lot of weight and was extremely depressed and nervous. I cried all the way home to Georgia. I moved to Columbus in July 2004 for the sole purpose of taking care of Mom.

Item 11.2

Judge Markley   March 19, 2010
Page 2

After Becky was convicted and then disappeared, Mom's health got really bad. Her neurologist said she had suffered two minor strokes. A few months later, she was diagnosed with Alzheimers so I moved her in with us. She subsequently fell and broke her hip and is currently residing at Monterey Care Center. She doesn't understand "why" she can't come home and "why" I don't come to see her.

For the past six years, everything I have done has been for my mother's benefit! I am 66 years old and mom is almost 86. I'm the only one left to care for her.

I communicated with my sister, Rebecca Parrett, for two reasons:

(1.) I promised our older brother, the night before he died, that I would forgive Becky for being so very mean to me during her entire life and that I would look after her in his absence.

(2.) Mom was able to speak with Becky a few times by phone, she received two letters from her, and she read several e-mails which I printed for her.

Item 11.3

Judge Markley   March 19, 2010
Page 3

Simply "knowing" that Becky is still alive has, in my opinion, kept my mother alive.

I made a horrible mistake for which I am truly sorry.

Since my arrest, I have cooperated fully with the U.S. Marshals and will continue to do so until Becky is caught and sent to prison.

With all my heart, Judge Markley, I sincerely apologize to you and beg you to please allow me to continue as caretaker for my mother.

Respectfully,

Linda Case

Item 12.1

Sheri L. Kent
3905 State Street, Suite 7-330
Santa Barbara, CA 93105
805.683.5000 Voicemail
805.294.3573 Cell
614.307.6141 Local

April 4, 2010

Dear Family and Friends,

I am writing to you because I need your help. My husband Albert and I have been carrying a burden alone for the past nearly two months now. It is regarding my mother – Linda Case. If you are receiving this, it is because she is a family member, a friend, an associate, or you have some type of relationship with her as well.

The situation: this is a very long and complicated story. I won't go into details (I don't know many to begin with) but before I begin, let me ask you to ask yourself this question … if a family member or loved one of yours was in trouble would you help them? And if the police or other authority came to you and asked you about them and you thought they would not find out – would you lie to protect your loved one? Answer that truthfully to yourself and then look at this story through that perspective, please.

As some of you know and many do not, my Aunt Becky Parrett – my mom's sister – got herself into some trouble. She and several prominent members of the company she founded were found guilty of numerous counts of securities fraud and other corporate fraud. All of the other members who were found guilty are now in prison. The presiding judge – Judge Marbley – showed compassion to them all and let them have some time to take care of their affairs before sending them to jail. True to character, my aunt did not act honorably and instead took off. She is now a fugitive. The US Marshall's Office has been looking for her for over two years now. Well, apparently Becky had set up a way for my mom to e-mail her and also had a private cell phone number that they could speak on. At no time did mom ever know where Becky was, just that she was alive. So, in essence, mom communicated with her sister. She did so in the privacy of her own home. My mom has never been in any kind of trouble in her life, so she (naively) believed that she had a right to privacy in her home to communicate with her sister. However, since Becky was now a wanted fugitive mom's e-mails were watched and her home phone, work phone and cell phone conversations were listened to and recorded by the US Marshall's office. The Marshalls also paid mom a few visits at the house where mom spoke to them and lied. Although she did not know where Becky was she also said that she had not heard from her – that they had not communicated with each other. So, on February 12th of this year the US Marshalls arrested my mom for obstruction of justice and providing false information – one count each. The obstruction charge has been dropped. Mom has been in jail ever since – so going on 8 weeks now. Albert and I were in Ohio at the time because we were helping mom go through things and get ready to take an RV trip with us to Mexico. Albert and I have been planning and saving for this trip for over 3 years now. He hasn't seen his family in over 10 years and I have never met my in-laws so it was long overdue. My mom has a good lawyer who is working hard to get her out of jail and have the least amount of sentencing possible. Can you imagine – she has already done almost 2 months in jail for a lie, it has cost her nearly $20,000 in legal fees and she is still in jail and looking at being sentenced to possible time in prison? My grandmother is in Monterey Care Center with progressing Alzheimer's disease and knows nothing about what has happened to my mom (thank goodness.) But Albert and I have been here in Ohio far longer than we planned, with no jobs, no family or friends, no support. Since she was put in jail we have been taking care of her dog and 4 cats, grandma's 3 cats that she was also caring for, her house, bills, income tax clients, etc. We have put our lives on hold to help her out and make sure that grandma continues to get the care that she needs as well. This has been extremely hard. Some days I feel like I am going to have a nervous breakdown but then I remind myself just how many people are counting on me to stay strong – grandma, Albert, 10 cats, a dog and of course – my mom.

In speaking with her lawyer he seems to think that personal letters to the judge will help my mom's case tremendously. **That's where you come in**. If you have anything kind to say about my mother and her relationship with you can you please write a letter to the judge and send it to me? I will give all the letters to her lawyer and he will pass them on to the judge to review before mom's sentencing. It doesn't have to be a long, fancy letter – just your truth about mom – maybe a story you can share about how she was thoughtful to you in some way or how she helped you or her professionalism in dealing with your taxes – anything positive. The Prosecuting Attorney and the judge in this case were the same ones that were involved with Becky's corporate fraud case – so that hasn't been good for mom. Becky, who was sentenced to 25 years in prison hasn't served one day in jail and my mom – who is guilty of keeping in touch with her – has already been there for 2 months. My mom has cooperated fully with the US Marshalls office and Prosecuting Attorney and will continue to do so – for all of our sakes.

For your conscious and information – I did ask mom "WHY" she did this, especially given how Becky has treated her over the years. She told me she did it for grandma. Grandma still believes that Becky is innocent and just got mixed up with the wrong crowd. A mother's love! Grandma's health suffered tremendously during the trial and especially once Becky disappeared. Grandma's doctor thinks she suffered at least two minor strokes. Mom sincerely believed that just knowing that her daughter was alive helped with grandma's health. And grandma got to talk to Becky a few times and got to read a few e-mails that she wrote.

Today is Easter Sunday. Families everywhere are together giving thanks and sharing time and making happy memories. Albert and I are all alone in Ohio, his family is still waiting for us to join them in Mexico, my grandmother is in the care center and mom is in jail. Can you please help us?

If you can write something on mom's behalf just address the letter to: The Honorable Judge Algenon Marbley and send it to me at:

Sheri Kent
4954 Demorest Drive
Grove City, OH 43123

If you can't find anything in your heart to say about my mom, then please pray to whomever you pray to for her and for Albert, grandma and me.

If you would like to write to my mom:

Linda Case #41099
c/o Delaware County Jail
844 US Hwy 42 N
Delaware, OH 43015

THANK YOU!!!

Item 12.2

Below is a copy of what I wrote to the judge:

"Dear Judge Marbley:

My name is Sheri Kent. I am Linda Case's daughter. I want to tell you a little bit about my mom ... a few things about her character and who she is as a person that might help you discern mom's sentence.

First, let me say how much it pains me to see that this matter is regarding **The United States of America vs. my mother**. That seems very unlikely – if you knew her. My mom spent the majority of her married years *serving this country* by being a military wife. My father - Arthur Kent - served two terms in the Air Force and one term in the Army. They were stationed at Tinker Air Force Base in Oklahoma City, OK when my dad went overseas to assist with the Vietnam War. My mom spent her entire pregnancy with me alone – and even gave birth by herself. I didn't meet my father until I was hospitalized (and nearly died) at 3 months old and my father was allowed to return home to see me. Now that is a *sacrifice* FOR your country! Mom was married to dad about 8 years and then later married Kenniston Case – my stepfather. He was in the active National Guard and (like my father) was stationed somewhere new every couple of years. So, every couple of years my mom had to pick up and pack up and relocate herself and her family to a new part of this country to support my father and then subsequently my stepfather so they could serve this country. That's how my mom served this country – and that is how I served this country. This is not an easy life for the spouses and children but we were *proud to be*

American and happy to sacrifice and do what we could. This meant that we never had a place that we could call "home" for very long. We spent a lot of time on army and air force bases around this country as well as attending military functions. I can't tell you how many times we heard the speeches that started "Duty, Honor, Country ..." and every time how satisfied we all felt at being a part of something so great. My mom is very *patriotic and loves this country* very much and has sacrificed a lot personally for it. I hope that is taken into consideration with regard to her sentencing.

I would like to share you with some examples that illustrate my mom's character and personality.

She is a regular person. She is a *proud Ohio State alumnus,* she loves to watch Ohio State football, she enjoys playing bridge and has played for many years with the Central Ohio Bridge Association over on Bethel Rd, she enjoys organic gardening, movies, Dancing With The Stars, American Idol and Donatos pizza.

She is a very *generous* and *compassionate* woman often *volunteering* her time at the McDowell Senior Center to help seniors with their tax questions and has volunteered at the Capital Area Humane Society. She adores animals. She is *kind, warm and empathetic.* Even though she doesn't have much – she is always giving something to someone, whether it is household items to the Kidney Foundation, a donation to help the homeless with their Thanksgiving meals, newspapers to the dog shelter, money to the Humane Society and ASPCA or donating used cell phones, women's clothing and accessories to shelters for battered and abused women.

She is *intelligent and accomplished.* I would like to add – my mom never graduated from high school.

Her parents were simple West Virginia country folks; my grandfather was a carpenter who didn't finish high school and my grandmother was a nurse's aid who didn't finish high school. However, in spite of her background mom went on to get her GED and be ***the first college graduate from either side of the family!*** I was attending college myself at the time and was so proud to watch her walk across the stage at OSU and accept her diploma. This was not easy for her because it took her 7 years because she was working full time, supporting herself and raising two teenage daughters alone. But she didn't give up. When she sets her mind to something she can accomplish it. After that, she established and built a very *successful* small business here in Columbus doing income taxes and bookkeeping for other small businesses. I learned how to do accounting as her apprentice at Case Accounting & Tax Service. Mom taught me everything I needed to know – gave me the foundation, knowledge and experience to make a living and have a career in accounting. She provided a great service to her clients.

(I had to leave out the name of the business and person to protect their privacy.)

In 1996 my mom sold her business so that she could move closer to my brother and me and her grandchildren in California. She sold it to a partnership named XX. Part of the deal was that after a down payment, mom would work for X for one tax season and transition all of her clients over to the new owners. Then, after she moved, they were to send payments after every tax season for several years until they had paid off the full amount. My mom kept her end of the contract. However, after moving to CA she was notified that they would not be sending any more payments. One of the partners – Mr. X – had contracted AIDS and was very ill. My mom was devastated. She was counting on that money for her future, her retirement. She was entitled to that money because she worked hard for many years to build her business and clientele to what it was when she sold it. Was her decision to hire a lawyer and legally pursue her deserved, contracted payments? No. My mom chose to walk away. What kind of a person would sue someone who is sick? As an after-note, Mr. X is alive and well and owns a lovely home in Victorian Village and is still reaping the rewards (which he never paid for) from what my mom sowed. Even after returning to Columbus my mom has honored her part of their contract with regard to the "non-compete" part and wishes him no ill will. That story shows extreme *honor*, *character* and compassion.

My mom is a very *fun, sociable* part of any community – whether it is family or geographical. When she was living in Santa Ynez, CA she was the Business Administrator for the Santa Ynez Valley Presbyterian Church and also a member of the Santa Ynez Valley Chamber of Commerce and Women's Club. She helped organize the singles group at the church and other activities. After returning home to Columbus she has been involved with the local senior center, has taken clogging lessons and even some other ballroom dancing lessons. She is a very active "senior" citizen.

Judge, I waited until I was 36 years old and found the right man before I got married. The man I happened to fall in love with was of Mexican descent. Honestly, there were quite a few members of my family who did not accept Albert at first, including both my mother and father. They come from rural West Virginia and there wasn't much diversity there. But, after coming to know my husband's heart and character the person who has accepted him the most has been my mom. Only she and my sister even acknowledged our marriage at first. Now, my mom is learning Spanish so that when she visits our in-laws in Mexico she can communicate with them in their own language. Mom really is *amazing*. Once she learns something she tenaciously wants to learn more and integrates that knowledge into who she is. Knowing Albert has helped her learn to be a more *open minded, tolerant* person. She is one of only a few family members that I have an actual relationship with – and not just see during holidays, special occasions or funerals. Even though she is in jail she is the only one who has remembered Albert's and my anniversary. Tomorrow we have been married 7 years. Mom is also a very *thoughtful* person. Even amidst her current circumstances she sent us a card she bought on her account at the commissary at Delaware County. We really want her to be a part of our lives. Albert and I have a lot of faith in her. Like everyone, she makes mistakes. But I can tell you that she also makes HUGE recoveries.

One of mom's dominant roles has always been that of *caregiver*. Over the years she has rescued countless dogs and cats and has had an "open door" policy with her home with respect to any family member who needed a place to stay while they were getting their life together. I have been a big beneficiary of that generosity over the years – regardless of how old I was. If I needed a place to stay mom was there with open arms and a welcoming smile. She has also let my sister Trisha and her first husband Smith and child Aaron move in and stay with her while they were in the process of relocating back to Columbus after Smith's time in the Marine Corps ended. They stayed with mom for several months in her small two-bedroom condo and mom also helped with babysitting while they had interviews and provided other vital assistance to them while they were segueing back into civilian life. Just several years ago this same grandson – Aaron – who was then living with Trisha and her second husband Tom in Buford, GA came to stay with my mom. He was very much a typical "troubled teen", very rebellious of authority, doing drugs, stealing things, running away from home. My sister felt like she couldn't handle him anymore. After the last time he ran away and was gone for 2-3 weeks (I think) his only option was to go to military school or come up and live with my mom. Aaron decided to come up and live with my mom – his grandma. He was with my mom for over a year and the improvement was incredible. He made friends and became more sociable, he made the honor roll nearly every time at Grove City High School, he enrolled in the ROTC program and was one of their most promising cadets, he played rugby and graduated from Grove City High School. Mom helped him in so many ways. She set aside her own desires and really put a lot of time and love and energy into this kid. She helped him learn to drive; she assisted him with college applications and scholarship applications. She *GIVES* a lot of herself to her family – most importantly – to my grandmother – mom's mother. Grandma is a very independent and stubborn woman. Physically, she is pretty healthy for an 86-year-old woman. However, grandma has been diagnosed with Alzheimer's disease and it is getting progressively worse. Grandma was living on her own in her house in Valley view until October of 2008. I came back to Columbus from Santa

Barbara and helped move my grandma in with my mom – so mom would be able to care for her. Grandma needs 24 hour care. She doesn't think she does but she will go out and try and shovel the driveway and hurt herself or walk on the ice to get the mail and fall down and hit her head or set the house alarm off and not remember how to turn it off or have the heat set at 85 degrees during the summer. These types of things were happening on a daily basis. So it was time. While grandma was here with mom she slipped in the kitchen and fell and broke her hip. She had to have surgery and now does have some difficulty walking – although she can manage with her cane and a little help. It breaks my mom's heart that grandma is in Monterey Care Center and not at home. Mine too. Mom was retiring this year so she could bring grandma home and devote the majority of her time to taking care of her. I sincerely hope that this will also be taken into consideration when considering my mom's sentence.

Mom is also a very *conscientious, thoughtful* person. She cares about not just herself and her family and community but this country and this planet. A lot of the decisions she makes, i.e. recycling, planting organic, never wasting anything, etc. are because she believes she has a caretaker responsibility as well. She brought me up to be a conscientious person too. We haven't been able to speak in detail about the circumstances that landed her in jail. But, she has told me and everyone else how sorry she is and that once she is able to she will do everything she can for the rest of her life to make this right for all of us. I believe she will.

My mom has had an especially hard time with the loss of my brother Mike (her son) who passed away in September of 1998. Since then she has also lost her father, her stepfather, her brother and her best friend. Grandma's Alzheimer's has taken a big part of her away as well. I think my mom is still grieving these losses and this grief may have clouded her judgment with respect to my Aunt Becky Parrett – who is one of mom's few remaining immediate family members. They did not have much of a relationship at all for years. My aunt is not a nice person and my mom and her have virtually nothing in common except genes and their childhoods. However, when my uncle Dannie died in November of 2002 he asked my Aunt Becky to apologize to members of this family – including my mom and me – for her past transgressions. He also asked mom to promise him she would look after Becky. These were his last requests – his deathbed wishes. My mom was honoring this promise to her brother. She knows what she did for Becky is wrong and has *cooperated fully* with the US Marshall's office, Drew Shadwick in particular, and Doug Squires the Prosecuting Attorney. And she will continue to cooperate and do exactly what is expected of her – for all of our sakes.

Except for my grandmother – who still believes Becky was innocent and just "in with the wrong crowd" (mother's love!) - the rest of our family believes that she is guilty of far more than she was convicted of; far worse crimes because they are crimes of the heart, crimes against the spirits of the people who love you. She is and has been an embarrassment to us all for a long time. I can speak for the entire family when I say that we want nothing more than for her to be captured and serve her sentence. That will be justice for all of her victims from the corporate fraud that she was convicted of.

However, with regard to my aunt, there can never be reparations or justice with what she has done to this family or what she has put us through. I meditate and pray every day a lot about this situation. I pray that the part of Becky that is human – the part that connects her to all of us, all of humanity – cries out to her conscious to do the right thing and turn herself in. I pray that my grandma won't pass away before we can bring her home from the care center. I pray that Albert's and my finances and marriage hold out during this tumultuous time while we are here in Ohio taking care of mom's responsibilities until we can get back to leading our lives. I pray that someday my entire family will be able to put the past behind us, communicate lovingly, heal and trust each other again. I pray for your compassionate discernment of my mom's unique case. I pray for Mr. Squire's compassionate discernment as well. My mom is not my aunt. And I pray that my mom will survive in jail until you sentence her and she can come home. I pray and hope that her sentence will be for "time served" and if necessary probation and possibly some counseling. I give thanks and am grateful for Mr. Smith – my mom's lawyer. He has been a great help and tremendous comfort to our family during this very trying time. And, I am very grateful for all of the professionalism and empathy shown to my family and my mom in particular from Drew Shadwick of the US Marshall's office. I have spoken with him more over the past 7 weeks than any of my best friends. I have wholeheartedly volunteered my help in any way that will help bring my aunt to justice or help with my mom's case.

Ironically, my mom has suffered the most at Becky's hand throughout her life and she is still suffering. My grandmother told us that when all of her kids were little that Becky would do bad things to my uncle and my mother. Then at the end of the day – when it was time to go to bed – Becky would be scared to go to sleep if everyone she wronged during the day didn't forgive her. Instead of punishing my aunt for doing bad things - my uncle and my mom were actually punished if they didn't forgive her. Although I am not a psychiatrist, I believe this part of their upbringing was crucial to both of them. Becky learned that there were no consequences for her actions and my mom learned that if she didn't forgive Becky she would be punished. I do believe in forgiveness. I forgive my mom and I hope that you, Mr. Squires, Mr. Shadwick and the rest of the United States of America (the part involved in this case anyway) can forgive my mother as well.

My father passed away New Year's Day 2005. Even though they were divorced – my mom and dad remained friends throughout his life. At my father's funeral my mom was the only person who spoke about him – other than my sister. It must have been hard for her to stand up at the microphone – in front of her ex in-laws - and speak about my dad, but she did it for me. She shared some very loving stories that I'm sure no one in the family had ever heard – not even me – about their time together. It helped begin the healing process for me, although my grief would continue for some time afterwards. Imagine the *courage* that it must have taken. That's the kind of person my mother is.

For the record, mom does have a plan. Once she is allowed out of jail she wants to move into grandma's house in Valleyview and then bring grandma home and take care of her there. The house is paid for so my mom should be able to take care of my grandmother and them both live comfortably. My husband Albert and I are prepared to move their belongings over there for them once we get the "green light" from the court that she is coming home. We have been staying at the house in Grove City and taking care of mom's 4 cats, mom's dog, grandma's 3 cats, the house, and various other tasks associated with running a household AND keeping up with grandma since mom was incarcerated on February 12th – 7 weeks ago. We are obviously very anxious for her to return safely home to us - as well as her responsibilities - so that we can all resume our lives.

I would like to add just a little more to what I have said about my relationship with my mom. My mom gave me life. She has nurtured me, taken care of me, taught me right from wrong, disciplined me when I needed it, cried with me during my heartbreaks, laughed with me at my joys, celebrated with me at my victories, challenged me to be better when I could be, helped me when I needed it and loved me no matter what. She isn't perfect, but none of us are. She is one of the great loves of my life and I miss her tremendously. And, I worry about her being in the environment that she is in at 66 years old. So, on behalf of myself, my husband Albert, my grandma Nellie, mom's dog Sonny Boy, her cats Willie, Patsy, Elvis Pussly and Demi Mewer, grandma's cats Tommy, Baby and Donna can you please let my mom come home to us soon?

Please feel free to contact me anytime if you need anything further or have any questions or require clarification. I am available and happy to help in any way that I can.

Thank you very much! I appreciate your time and will continue to pray for blessings for you and your family.

Sincerely, Sheri Kent

Item 13

May 7, 2010

Ms Linda
Even on this special day
There No words
One can say
to replace the sound of your childs voice
or pick out a mothers day's gift
of their choice
But you need to Know
even though
Your here seperated from your children
a wonderful journey is about to begin
Your wisdom, Knowledge and sharing
has taught many the meaning of caring
Your loved and respected
and this Mothers day
your Not to be forgotten or negleted
but apprecnated, valued and loved
And reminded this situation bestowed
upon you
will not last forever –
And you – a wonderful mother, friend & confidant
are wished you get everything you want
I know this poem isent much
yet hope it adds the needed touch
to fill your heart with a little joy and laughter
and Keep your spirits high
for many days after! HAPPY Mothers DAY!
Shelly Slocum

Item 14.1

Fugitive financier's sister sentenced to 6 months

Business First

Date: Friday, July 9, 2010, 2:55pm EDT

The sister of fugitive financier Rebecca Parrett has been sentenced to six months in prison on charges that she lied to investigators searching for the former **National Century Financial Enterprises Inc.** executive.

U.S. District Court Judge Algenon Marbley sentenced Linda L. Case, 66, on Friday. She's been behind bars since her arrest in February and will receive credit for the time spent, Marbley's office said.

In addition to the jail time, Case is required to spend eight months under house arrest with an ankle monitoring device, followed by three years of probation. Prosecutors have dropped an obstruction of justice charge as part of an agreement Case struck to plead guilty to a count of willfully making a false statement.

Case is the sister of Parrett, a former National Century executive who disappeared a year ago and believed by the government to be hiding in Mexico. Case was taken into custody in February at her Grove City residence and later waived her rights to a detention hearing and preliminary trial.

Parrett has been missing since shortly after her March 2008 conviction on nine counts of fraud, conspiracy and money laundering stemming from the 2002 collapse of Dublin-based National Century. She was sentenced in absentia last March to 25 years in prison.

Item 14.2

Columbus Dispatch 7-10-2010

NATIONAL CENTURY

Fugitive's sister sent to prison for lying

Mexico rendezvous planned with former exec, e-mails show

By Kathy Lynn Gray
THE COLUMBUS DISPATCH

A federal government attempt to reel in fugitive Rebecca S. Parrett by charging her 66-year-old sister with obstruction hasn't panned out so far.

The sister, Linda Case of Grove City, was sent to prison yesterday while Parrett remains free, probably in Mexico.

Linda Case, 66, was sentenced to six months in prison.

U.S. District Judge Algenon L. Marbley sentenced Case to six months in prison, followed by eight months of house arrest and three years of probation after she is released. Case will receive credit for the four months she has spent in jail.

"I accept full responsibility for lying," she said in court. "I'm so very sorry."

See LYING Page B2

LYING

FROM PAGE B1

Marbley said he found it ironic that Case's "blind loyalty to an undeserving sister has caused (Case) to serve time" when that sister has yet to serve her prison term.

Parrett was sentenced last year in absentia to 25 years in prison for nine fraud-related convictions involving National Century Financial Enterprises, a company that provided financing to small health-care providers. Eleven people were convicted for taking money from the company and hiding the shortfall, taking down 275 health-care providers when NCFE went bankrupt in 2002.

U.S. marshals arrested Case in February on charges of obstruction of justice and lying to investigators. They said she had been e-mailing Parrett regularly since Parrett disappeared after her trial in March 2008. Case pleaded guilty to one count of making false statements.

The criminal complaint against her, which was unsealed Thursday, said she and her sister had planned to meet in Mexico, where Parrett was living, after Case traveled there in an RV with her dog and seven cats. She told Parrett in e-mails that she planned to leave Ohio on Feb. 14, drive to Mexico in the RV, rent an apartment, then fly back to the U.S. to bring their ailing 66-year-old mother to Mexico.

Case repeatedly told in-

Rebecca S. Parrett was sentenced last year in absentia to 25 years for fraud.

vestigators in 2008 and 2009 that she hadn't had any contact with her sister, and she gave investigators false information about where her sister was.

The sentencing memorandum the government filed says "The fact that Parrett is still at-large highlights the impact of (the) defendant's false statements."

Assistant U.S. Attorney Douglas W. Squires said during yesterday's sentencing that since Case's arrest, she "has provided substantial assistance" to investigators.

Joseph E. Scott, Case's attorney, argued in court documents that Parrett took advantage of her sister's kind-heartedness.

"Ms. Parrett has a history of manipulating people and situations for her own benefit," Scott wrote in a sentencing memorandum for Case. "During the days when Ms. Parrett was making an outrageous amount of money as a result of her company, Ms. Parrett simply ignored her family and treated them like 'West Virginia's hillbillies.'"

Case began e-mailing Parrett after her disappearance to reassure their mother that Parrett was alive, the memorandum says.

kgray@dispatch.com

Linda Case and sister Becky in 1951

Mom

Dan, Linda and Becky

Albert and Sheri

Grandson Aaron and Sonny Boy

Made in the USA
San Bernardino, CA
27 September 2016